Nonfiction:

FROM IDEA TO PUBLISHED BOOK

Nonfiction:

FROM IDEA TO
PUBLISHED BOOK

Harry Edward Neal

Wilfred Funk, Inc.
New York

0 29. 6
N 339

Excerpts from other books by the author are reprinted through the courtesy
of the following publishers—

Chilton Company:

The Hallelujah Army: The Salvation Army in Action.

Julian Messner, Inc.:

Communication: From Stone Age to Space Age
Diary of Democracy: The Story of Political Parties in America
Disease Detectives: Your Career in Medical Research
Engineers Unlimited: Your Career in Engineering
From Spinning Wheel to Spacecraft: The Story of the Industrial Revolution
Money Masters: Your Career in Banking
Nature's Guardians: Your Career in Conservation
Pathfinders, U.S.A.: Your Career on Land, Sea and Air
Six Against Crime: Treasury Agencies in Action
Treasures by the Millions: The Story of the Smithsonian Institution
Your Career in Electronics

"Editors' and Proofreaders' Marks" reprinted by
permission of the Mergenthaler Linotype Company

To Helen with love

Preface

To become a professional writer you don't have to be:

> A college graduate
> Young
> Eccentric
> Starving

You should be:

> Literate
> Curious
> Enthusiastic
> Persevering

Take me, for instance. I never finished high school. I had no thought of writing for publication until I was thirty-seven years old. In 1926 I entered the United States Secret Service as a stenographer and was assigned to the New York District, where I worked until 1940 (I was commissioned a Secret Service Agent in 1931).

In 1940 I was transferred to Secret Service headquarters in Washington as a member of the chief's staff. Frank J. Wilson, chief at that time, was beginning a "Know Your Money" campaign designed to show retail storekeepers how to detect counterfeit bills and coins, on the theory that those armed with such knowledge would not easily be victimized by passers of fake money. As part of this campaign Chief Wilson asked me to write an article for a trade journal explaining the differences between genuine and bogus currency.

I knew a great deal about counterfeiting, but little about writing for publication. My writing had been confined to official correspondence, investigative reports in criminal cases, management and annual reports, prosecution reports, and other documents incident to Secret Service work. I wrote the article, which was published under the chief's by-line. When editors of other retailers' trade magazines saw it and wrote to the chief requesting similar pieces for their publications, he referred their letters to me. It was then that I decided I'd better learn something about professional writing, although I still had no thought of writing under my own name.

At American University in Washington, D.C., I took a night course, Applied Government Writing, conducted by William Dow Boutwell, a wise and visionary teacher who is now Director of the Teen-Age Book Club associated with Scholastic Magazines, Inc. I am deeply indebted to Bill Boutwell, not only for his teaching and guidance, but also for encouraging me to maintain my interest in writing.

When the Boutwell course ended, there was one other open —a course, Writing the Short Story, given by Professor Merritt C. Batchelder. I had no special interest in fiction, but I enrolled for the course on the theory that *whatever* I learned

about writing would be helpful to me in my work. Dr. Batchelder was also a fine teacher who became my good friend, and it was in his class that I became so interested in fiction writing that I resolved to try some short stories on my own—none, however, having to do with the Secret Service.

One Sunday, while I was still taking the course, I read a newspaper advertisement that gave me an idea for a "short-short" story—a form that looks easy but I now know is the hardest of all to write. I wrote a 1,000-worder and sent it to *Holland's* magazine. Back came a check for $20—my first fiction sale! I was so fired up that I told my wife I ought to quit my Secret Service job and write stories. This one had been written in an hour or so, and I figured that I could produce eight stories every eight-hour day, which, at twenty bucks each, would bring a neat $160 a day.

Luckily my wife talked me out of writing for a living, but I was now confident that I had the *ability* to write salable stuff. On this basis my wife and I agreed that I would enter into a five-year plan. After writing for five years, if I had not made some significant progress (meaning several major sales), I'd write "good-by" on the typewriter and leave the field to the real craftsmen.

I wrote almost every night and every Saturday and Sunday. During the year following my sale to *Holland's,* I wrote nearly ninety stories and articles, none of which sold. But I know now, and have known for a long time, that I served my *real* writing apprenticeship in that year. I collected hundreds of rejection slips, all of which I considered to be something like Boy Scout merit badges. As soon as I finished one magazine piece I'd put it in the mail and begin another. I sent manuscripts to all of the big slick magazines, and the big

slick magazines sent 'em right back. But sometimes they were accompanied by encouraging notes from editors, and these brief scribbles were almost as exciting as acceptance checks.

Then one day I received a cordial letter from Miss Lillian Genn, article editor of *Argosy* magazine. In effect, she said, "I've been watching your stuff come across my desk for lo these many months, and I think it's pretty good. I also think that you ought to work with a literary agent."

I thanked Miss Genn for her extraordinary kindness and said that I would be delighted to work with a literary agent if she could recommend a reliable one who would be willing to market my material. She did even more. She talked with Mrs. Leslie Gordon Phillips, who conducted an agency with an associate, Patricia Lewis, and they agreed to look at my work. (Miss Lewis, who now conducts the agency, is still my representative.)

I sent the agents a short story that had been rejected by twelve magazines. "If you don't want to sell this story," I wrote, "send it back to me because I'll sell it if I have to send it to twelve *hundred* magazines!"

Mrs. Phillips said the story was good, and just about one week after she received it she sold it to *Esquire*. More sales followed—to *Collier's, Cosmopolitan, Coronet, Pageant, Saga, The Saturday Evening Post, Family Circle, American Girl, Blue Book, Liberty, Argosy, Christian Herald,* and *The Writer,* among others.

Later I made good use of my huge collection of rejection slips, all of which I had saved. When my first book was published (*Writing and Selling Fact and Fiction,* Wilfred Funk, Inc., New York, 1949), I was invited to talk about it during

a week-long book fair sponsored by the Washington Arts Club.

I said to my wife, "All week there will be talks by well-known authors at this fair. Nobody knows me, with my one lone book. We've got to think of something that will help to make my talk outstanding, so I won't show up too badly against the big competition."

"Maybe you could shoot a pencil out of some writer's mouth," she suggested.

"Too noisy," I said.

I finally bought a long roll of ribbon to which my wife and I stapled a few hundred rejection slips. On the day of my talk I brought the decorated ribbon along in a suitcase. I spoke to the audience about my book and concluded by saying, "Now I'm going to *show* you—not just tell you—what it takes to become a writer."

I opened the suitcase, handed one end of the ribbon to a surprised man in the front row, and unfolded it carefully as I walked across the platform until all the rejection slips were in view, like laundry on a clothesline.

"These," I said proudly, "are my rejection slips!"

The act brought down the house, and at the week's end I received a telephone call from the club secretary who said, "I thought you'd like to know that we sold more copies of your book than any other at the fair."

The book is still in print, still selling.

After devoting thirty-one years of my life to the Secret Service, in which I reached the position of assistant chief, I had the opportunity to write several books, but I couldn't do the necessary research and also keep my law-enforcement job, so I had to make a choice. After a conference with my wife,

Helen, and my children, Barbara and Harry, Jr., I decided to retire from the government and devote my full time to free-lance writing, which I now do.

I write very little magazine material today because most of my time is spent in researching and writing nonfiction books. The one you are now reading is my eighteenth to be published, and others are in progress.

Many of the eighteen were published by Julian Messner, Inc., New York, where I have enjoyed a cordial working relationship with Editor Gertrude Blumenthal, whose suggestions and guidance have invariably led to improvements in my book manuscripts.

I have told you all this for two reasons—to show that you *can* travel the road to writing success despite its rocks and holes, and to acquaint you with my qualifications for writing this book.

I hope that you will find it helpful.

—H. E. N.

Loghaven,
Rixeyville, Virginia

Contents

Nonfiction:

FROM IDEA TO PUBLISHED BOOK

1

Starting Points

As a writer you could make a million dollars.

You *could*—but the chances are that you never will!

However, that's a nice round figure to keep in mind as a goal—provided, of course, that you write (or intend to write) for money.

Writing for money is considered in some quarters to be a prostituted art, but even those who so believe are not averse to writing for money in this fashion: "Dear Uncle Herkimer: Will you please send me four hundred bucks pending the arrival of the gold train?"

The man or woman who puts words together for sale is compelled to meet stiff competition from others who are doing exactly the same thing, including not a few whose financial returns must feed, clothe, and shelter themselves and their families. In other words, writing that begets money from publishers can't be slipshod or inferior; it is aimed at

1

a specific reading audience and it has to match the quality of that produced by skillful competitors. It has to be *good.*

This certainly doesn't mean that people who write for other reasons are foolish, although the written word, like all art, is meant to communicate, and if it lies buried in a bureau drawer or some other household grave, then it fails in this vital mission.

Perhaps you write for pure self-enjoyment; many people do.

Maybe you write (diaries, for instance) to keep memories alive, or even as a mental catharsis. In World War II, an American soldier in the Pacific kept a diary of his activities, simply for his own information. In 1963 it was published in book form and showed signs of becoming a best seller. The author is a garbage collector in New York City.

Or do you write "for art's sake" or some other reason that is especially meaningful to you?

POINT: *Decide in your own mind why you write or want to write, because there's a difference between writing and* being a writer. *If you're literate you can write what you please, when you please, for whom you please; but you won't be a* writer *until and unless you do the hard work that professional writing demands.*

WHAT KIND OF HARD WORK?

To become a published writer you must write. Not now and then, but regularly, and not just a paragraph or two, but thousands and thousands of paragraphs. In addition you must read, not only about current events, but also about history, science, the humanities, people. Read newspapers, magazines,

books, always studying the work of published writers—and write and write and write!

If this seems a gloomy outlook, it is an accurate one, but if you really want to be a writer you'll willingly suffer the slings and arrows of outrageous rejections and dejections and eventually discover that you have become a member of the professional writing fraternity.

THERE'S ALWAYS AN EXCUSE

Many writers, both professional and amateur, have become professional excuse inventors. One stares at a blank sheet of paper for ten minutes and suddenly decides to repair a faucet that has been leaking since Aunt Jezebel slipped in the bathtub eighteen months ago. One who's having trouble cutting 4,000 words out of a too-lengthy manuscript develops an irresistible urge to cut a lawn that wife, son, or husband mowed two days earlier.

Plumbing fixtures, lawnmowers, paint brushes, unwashed windows, personal letters, garden weeds—these are but a few of the evasions frequently chosen by the procrastinating writer who has word trouble. Sometimes, of course, a change of pace is beneficial. A brief interruption during a complex writing chore may become a problem-solver or at least help to clarify one's thinking, but if the interruption is a deliberate ruse to avoid writing, it's a weakness, a submission to temptation. And for what? It can't last forever. The moment must come when the writer says bravely "I shall return!", and marches back to his task.

The worst of all such evasions, in my opinion, is the one that goes, "I just don't have time." This is the tried, trite,

and untrue excuse offered by scores of men and women who *think* they want to be writers, but who really can't or won't muster the rigid self-discipline needed to produce the pages and pages of words that stack up to success. If you want to be a writer you *find* time for writing, even if it amounts to only fifteen minutes a day, *every day*.

Consider my own schedule, for example. I write two, sometimes three books a year, and perhaps an occasional magazine piece. When I'm doing research I put in a full eight-hour day, perhaps more. When my research is complete and it's time to begin writing, I go to work about eight-thirty in the morning and usually write at least four hours a day, excepting Saturdays and Sundays. I have contract deadlines to meet, so I can't dawdle, though I would so often much rather swim or fish in the river just outside my door, or hike through the woods, or read.

POINT: *It's always easy to find excuses for not writing. Avoid them. Admittedly self-discipline is one of the most difficult essentials of a writing career, but its maintenance is the mark of the true professional. As a writer, don't wait for inspiration or mood. Professional writing is a business, and to be businesslike you write regularly whether you feel inspired or not. If you don't want to be a professional (published) writer, remember that writing for yourself alone can be fun and sometimes unexpectedly rewarding.*

YOU CAN DO IT

Since you are reading this book I assume you are seriously interested in writing. You may be a beginner with little or no knowledge of book-writing techniques, or a persistent

writer with a drawer full of magazine rejection slips and little or no published work to your credit. Or maybe you have had some success in magazine writing and want to enter the book field. Whatever your status, you are apparently seeking more knowledge about writing.

When my book *Writing and Selling Fact and Fiction* was first published I sent a copy to my friend, William Hazlett Upson, best known as the creator of *The Saturday Evening Post* stories about Alexander Botts, the Earthworm tractor salesman. I sent the copy, not because I felt that any of my advice would be useful to Bill Upson, a truly successful author, but as a courtesy because the book included a short quotation from one of his magazine pieces. Subsequently I received a cordial letter in which Mr. Upson said that he had not only enjoyed reading my book, but also that it had brought out several basic principles that he had forgotten. "If you are wise," he said, "you'll take my advice and read your own book once in a while."

So if you're a professional, you may find that *this* book will freshen your mind about certain basics, or even lead to new or improved working methods.

Maybe you're a homemaker, with or without crib-size babies or school-age youngsters. Perhaps you live in a city apartment or a split-level suburban home, or in a white clapboard farmhouse near the mountains or on the prairie. Where you live doesn't matter so much as how you use your living time. "Living time" is now, this minute and the one coming up. All those other minutes, the ones that slipped away, are "dead time" and will never live again. How many of yours were purposeful or productive, so far as writing is concerned?

Many homemakers are successful writers and many others hope to be. Writing is an ideal activity for the homemaker because it can be fitted into the daily (or nightly) schedule at a time most convenient to the writer. It may be a vocation or an avocation, an income-getter or simply a means of relaxation.

I have several homemaker-writer friends. Among them is one wife and mother who keeps house in Connecticut and earns a comfortable income by writing books and magazine articles and by teaching classes in writing. Another, in Washington, D. C., shepherds a family of four in a big old frame house, writes books, a newspaper column, and magazine articles; she also gives lectures and teaches at writers' conferences. One young mother not only writes books for children, but also does the illustrations for them. Still another woman has a daily office job, maintains her home, and finds enough spare time to turn out books that provide a welcome supplement to her salary.

Most of these women are fairly young, but age is no obstacle to the man or woman who wants to be a writer. In fact, age can be a valuable asset because the elderly person can draw upon a wealth of experience, memories, and knowledge acquired through years of living—and this is a treasure not available to the young.

Are you a retired businessman (or woman), a senior citizen with time to garden, golf, fish, hunt, or pursue some other hobby? A lot of oldsters have found that writing can be enjoyable, instructive, and profitable. Oliver Wendell Holmes was at his creative peak in his sixties and seventies. Benjamin Franklin was still writing brilliantly in his eighties. Two of Mark Twain's books were written when he was past seventy.

Carl Sandburg, as he nears eighty-five, is still going great guns. W. Somerset Maugham, almost ninety, twice decided to "retire," but continues to write.

Writing also offers opportunity and fame to young people. Where the old have the past, the young have the future, which means that they have time to learn and work and grow. They are part of today's scientific revolution, part of the planning for tomorrow, and their possibilities for writing about our changing world are infinite.

One word of caution is important here. If you propose to make a career as a writer, you will be wise to prepare for it (that is, to write) in your spare time, and not to depend upon your writing for a livelihood until you have attained a rather high degree of success. Without a good supplemental income the average writer may be stuck for subsistence, impaled on his own free lance.

POINT: *Whoever you are, whatever you do, rich or poor, young or old, writing offers you a way to share your philosophy, acquire and impart new knowledge, meet interesting people, broaden your outlook, and earn extra money.*

WHAT EQUIPMENT DO YOU NEED?

As a writer you need a pen, pencil, or typewriter, paper, the will to work, a good vocabulary, and the ability to use it effectively.

It is not expected that the would-be professional writer will attempt to sell manuscripts unless and until he is reasonably well-grounded in the use of language. Poor sentence structure, poor punctuation, and bad spelling may impel an editor to reject material whose content may be of interest,

and editors have every right to expect that a professional writer knows how to use his tools, which are words.

If you are a beginning writer, perhaps with an interrupted formal education, you will find it to your great advantage to study grammatical rules and working principles while you practice your literary scales and before you attempt to market what you write. To most editors and publishers, a manuscript represents its author, and if the work abounds in misspellings, bad punctuation, mistakes in grammar, or is otherwise sloppy or second-rate, the writer is branded accordingly.

A shelf of reference books should be an important part of your writer's library. Most invaluable to the writer, of course, is a good dictionary—and one that has been recently revised. A dictionary published twenty years ago is about as much help to a writer in our age as a horse-driven plow is to a farmer. I personally like to use the Funk & Wagnalls *Standard College Dictionary,* which is a completely new and comprehensive desk-size dictionary. With a dictionary like this and a Roget's *Thesaurus,* you should be at no loss for words.

You will also make good use of a standard encyclopedia—*Funk & Wagnalls, Americana, Britannica, World Book,* or the one-volume *Columbia Encyclopedia.*

Here are a few other suggestions for stocking your reference shelf:

University of Chicago Style Manual
The New York *Times* Style Book
Information Please Almanac
Descriptive English Grammar, by Homer C. House and Susan E.
  Harman. Prentice-Hall, Inc., Englewood Cliffs, N. J., 1950.

English Grammar Simplified, by James C. Fernald, revised by Cedric Gale. Funk & Wagnalls, New York, 1963.

The Macmillan Handbook of English, by John M. Kierzek. The Macmillan Co., New York, 1954.

Hook's Guide to Good Writing, by J. N. Hook. Ronald Press, New York, 1962.

Familiar Quotations, by John Bartlett. Little, Brown & Co., Boston. (Latest edition).

Making Books Work: A Guide to the Use of Libraries, by Jennie M. Flexner. Simon & Schuster, New York, 1943.

Many helpful reference works are now available in inexpensive paperbound editions. Among these are:

Grammar, Rhetoric and Composition, by Richard D. Mallery. Doubleday & Co., New York, 1963.

Guide to the Use of Books and Libraries, by Jean Key Gates. McGraw-Hill, New York, 1963.

Roget's Pocket Thesaurus. Edited by C. O. Sylvester Mawson and Katharine Aldrich Whiting. Pocket Books, Inc., New York, 1950.

English Grammar, by George O. Curme. College Outline Series. Barnes & Noble, New York, 1953.

Punctuate it Right! by Harry Shaw. Everyday Handbooks. Barnes & Noble, New York, 1963.

If the suggested books about English grammar are not readily available, your local bookstore or public librarian can recommend one or two others that will be worth owning. You can build your reference library volume by volume, week by week, or month by month, according to your income.

POINT: *As a writer, words are your stock in trade. Learn how to use them properly and forcefully. Learn how to spell correctly. Learn how and where to use proper punctuation. (I*

once received a letter without punctuation; as a postscript the writer included two lines of punctuation marks and this sentence: "Please put these in where they belong!")

Remember!

- Decide whether you merely *want to write* or *want to be a writer,* and why.
- Resolve to work diligently at writing and reading—and don't cheat on your resolution!
- Don't invent excuses for not writing.
- Whether you are young, old, or in-between, male or female, you *can* be a writer.
- Be assured a living income before you depend upon writing for a livelihood.
- Build a good reference library.
- Above all, *write!*

2

Face the Facts

Some writers begin their literary careers by writing fiction —that is, short stories or novels.

Some begin by writing poetry.

Others, for a variety of reasons, feel more self-confident in producing magazine articles or factual books, both of which fall into a category that has come to be known as "nonfiction."

Why "nonfiction"? Why not be frank and forthright and place prose writing into two classes, fiction and fact? Failing that, why not call meat "nonpotatoes" and men "nonwomen"?

According to Funk & Wagnalls' *Standard College Dictionary*, the word *fiction* means "A division of literature consisting of prose works in narrative form, the characters and incidents of which are wholly or partly imaginary." The word *fact* means "Something asserted to be true or to have happened."

Nonfiction writers are expected to be nonliars, as distinguished from fiction writers, all of whom are professional fibbers. The fiction writer creates imaginary people and mythical situations, and the nonfiction writer reports what he actually sees, hears, learns, feels, smells, tastes, believes.

In other words, the fiction writer deals in make-believe and the nonfiction writer deals in cold, hard facts. Cold, hard facts, however, can often be made warm and soft and as exciting as make-believe by using certain techniques that we'll discuss in the pages ahead.

One question that has frequently been asked of me and of other writers is "Which is easier to write—fiction or nonfiction?"

The answer isn't easy, because it varies with individuals. I have done both, and for me nonfiction is easier to write than fiction.

I became a nonfiction writer soon after I learned the alphabet, when I wore knee pants and a Buster Brown collar. I can't remember all my early literary efforts, but one went something like this: "My dog is brown. My dog is big. His tail is tiny. His name is Bo. He wags it good."

This didn't shake any literary circles, nor did it bring a rejection slip. As the school years passed I wrote a number of "compositions" and learned about subjects, predicates, participles, nouns, verbs, adverbs, adjectives, infinitives, commas, semicolons, periods, paragraphs, and other essentials to literacy, including spelling. When I was sixteen I had to quit school, take a quickie (eight-month) business course, and go to work to earn my living, but I continued to read and learn in my spare time, as I still do.

Since my school days I have written social and business

letters, investigative reports, annual reports, press releases, documentary movie scripts, one or two recipes, scores of magazine articles, and a number of books, all consisting of collections of facts, facts, facts. I'm sure that you have also written school compositions, letters, and other documents, and this illustrates my point that every literate man, woman, and child is capable of fact writing and has produced some kind of "nonfiction," though perhaps not for pay.

Fiction writing requires the exercise of considerable imagination to populate a paper world with made-up characters in conflicts that are the phantom creations of living, breathing authors. As a nonfiction writer you will deal in facts that you collect from many sources, so your major problem will consist of selecting the most interesting, most significant facts, organizing these facts, and presenting them effectively in a manner that will inform, entertain, or stimulate the reader.

POINT: *The would-be fiction writer who may encounter insurmountable obstacles in trying to create a salable short story may still be successful in the writing of nonfiction. In either field, your task is to inform, entertain, or stimulate the reader. Try both fiction and fact. What can you lose?*

THE NONFICTION MARKET

Look at almost any popular national magazine—*The Saturday Evening Post, Cosmopolitan, Esquire, McCall's,* among others—and you will see from the table of contents that the number of pages devoted to factual articles is much greater than that of pages carrying fiction. Why? Because readers are intensely interested in what's going on in the world. They want to be informed about matters that have some bearing

upon their lives, their families, their homes, their futures. They want to learn how to safeguard or improve their health; how to simplify housekeeping; how to grow better vegetables and flowers; how to make more money; how to raise children; how to decorate home interiors; how to eat and lose weight; how to see the world on $5 a day; how to invest in stocks and bonds; how to buy a house or an automobile; how to make a success of marriage; how to start a small business without really trying; or perhaps how to trap a wife or husband painlessly.

Look at the advertisements for new books. Here, as in magazines, the accent is on fact rather than fiction. There are behind-the-scenes revelations about the White House by former employees. Movie stars bare their private lives. Politicians and statesmen write their memoirs (or have them ghost-written by well-paid professional writers). Scientists predict the future and historians squabble about the past. There are nonfiction books for both adults and children on every conceivable subject, and scores of new titles are published every year.

TAKE THE WRITE ROADS

In later chapters we'll dwell upon the writing of nonfiction books, but if you're a beginner in the fact-writing field you may be hesitant about a first plunge into a full-length book, and quite rightly. For this reason, some suggestions leading up to book writing are offered for your consideration.

Maybe you'll prefer to start with a daily journal of your personal activities (which may later become most useful), or perhaps you'll begin the way I did, by writing fillers for mag-

azines. Fillers are those short personal anecdotes or brief accounts of interesting and unusual facts and occurrences which fill space, usually at the end of an article and the bottom of a page in magazines such as *Reader's Digest.* Study them to learn how concise the writing is and how varied the material, then write a few and send them out.

After writing and selling a few fillers you can tackle longer articles, which will improve your facility with words, and longer articles can lead you down several opportunity paths.

You can often get into print by writing letters to newspaper editors about current events, or community needs and projects, or any subjects that would interest other people. One writer who began by sending humorous items to a New York City newspaper columnist is now a successful writer of television scripts in Hollywood.

Newspapers that publish book reviews may need book reviewers. Katherine Anne Porter, author of the best-selling *Ship of Fools* and numerous short stories, once earned her bread and butter as a book reviewer in New York City. If you are well-versed in a specific field, a newspaper editor might be glad to have you read and review new books in that field. Perhaps you're not a qualified expert but you have a good background in literature—perhaps you have read many fictional works, and are capable of telling not only what a new novel is about but also of giving a potential reader a fair and objective opinion as to the book's merits and inadequacies. If so, you may be a welcome addition to a newspaper's staff for reviewing fiction, with a resultant broadening of your own reading and writing interests.

Newspapers, of course, offer other writing opportunities, and many successful authors began their careers as newspaper

reporters. Clarence Budington Kelland worked twelve-hour shifts as a young reporter in Detroit, then devoted spare time *every day* to the writing of magazine stories—but seven long years went by before he sold a single line. James Thurber was a newspaper reporter who did spare-time writing before he went to work for *The New Yorker*. Ernest Hemingway, John Gunther, Mark Twain, among numerous others, were newspapermen before they wrote books. A newspaper in or near your home may have a reporter's job open for you at this moment.

Marjorie Holmes, of Washington, D. C., keeps house for her family of four, writes magazine articles and teen-age novels. She wrote some samples of a proposed newspaper column called *Of Love and Laughter* and convinced the editor of the Washington *Evening Star* that his readers would find them appealing. Today her popular column appears in the *Star* regularly. It is a simple, warm, and human account of family happenings and reminiscences, with occasional items of universal interest based on letters from readers who write to Marjorie about their personal experiences or reactions, or on local events or personalities Marjorie herself has seen or heard about.

Could your local newspaper use a new feature, written by you? Write a few samples, send or show them to the editor, and give your reasons why you believe your feature would interest his readers.

Are you a good speaker? Could you write interesting speeches for local politicians, civic leaders, industrialists and others? This is a kind of ghost-writing that can pay off for those who can do it well. You can write letters to your representatives in state and federal legislatures, to city officials and

industrialists, outlining your qualifications as a speech writer and asking for an opportunity to service them in that capacity.

One of the biggest fields for the nonfiction writer is that involving public relations and publicity, including advertising. Because of the terrific competition in industry and trade, publicity about manufactured goods is of the utmost importance to the maker and the seller. Virtually all big companies employ men and women as publicists, or public relations representatives, to spread the good word (don't call it propaganda!) about the companies and their products. The publicists write news releases about company personnel, improvements in or new uses for goods, feature articles for newspapers and magazines, and perhaps scripts for radio and television interviews or commercials.

Radio and television stations, incidentally, often hire writers to produce so-called "spot" announcements, commercials for local firms, news features or other material needed throughout the broadcast day.

Department stores and other retail firms employ men and women to write advertising copy designed to bring customers to buy merchandise. Study the ads in your local newspaper to learn the art of persuasion. Try writing a few yourself— and if this is your meat, show your samples and sell yourself to a store's advertising manager.

Many public relations people have educational backgrounds in science, economics, business administration, or some other specialty which qualifies them for special writing jobs in industry, and they may be required to write anything from a description of a new electronic doohickey to a stockholder's annual report or a simplified message about manu-

facturing for use in fifth-grade classrooms. If you are a specialist in some activity, capitalize on your knowledge and training by writing about your specialty.

If you have had articles published and are interested in public relations work, send examples of your printed material to the director of public relations or the director of personnel of a company such as General Electric, Westinghouse, General Motors, Ford, the Radio Corporation of America, United States Steel, or Western Union, and ask about existing possibilities for a public relations job for yourself. Include a personal description, outline your educational history, experience, and give your reasons for applying.

The United States government employs a great many men and women as "information specialists." As such, they provide information to the public about the workings of their agencies. They may be assigned to write feature articles, news releases, speeches, or other material of public interest, and to cooperate with newspaper, magazine, and book writers who are seeking information about some facet of the governmental operation.

These jobs are filled by eligibles who have met the necessary requirements. For information about these requirements and job openings, write the U. S. Civil Service Commission, Washington 25, D. C.

Closely allied to public relations is the field of advertising, another area of publicity. One way to break into this business is to seek a job with an advertising agency. If you live in or near a big city you will find a listing of "Advertising Agencies" in the Yellow Pages of the telephone directory. Write or visit one or more to inquire about job opportunities. If you have no local listing of agencies, you may be

able to obtain information about those located in your vicinity by writing to the American Association of Advertising Agencies, 200 Park Avenue, New York 17, New York.

Some advertising and public relations firms "farm out" writing jobs—that is, they pay outside writers to do certain tasks, such as writing a sales brochure for a mortician-customer on *How to Die Happy,* or for a drug manufacturer who wants the world to know that *Our Pills Can Cure All Ills.* If you can't land a regular job in an agency, ask for a chance to do a free-lance assignment. If the assignment is done well it may lead to others, and eventually to the position you want.

POINT: *Numerous employment possibilities that are open to the nonfiction writer can provide useful experience for a career in the nonfiction book field. Explore these possibilities. Any job that requires you to write regularly will improve the quality and depth of your writing and can serve as a steppingstone to your future as a free-lance author.*

Remember!

- Try your hand at writing both fiction and fact to learn which you do (and like) best. Nonfiction doesn't always require the high degree of imagination that fiction does.
- The market for nonfiction is big and growing.
- In preparation for writing nonfiction books, consider applying for jobs requiring the writing of newspaper features, book reviews, columns, speeches, publicity, advertising copy, radio and TV commercials, or other printed matter.

3

Get the Idea

Nathaniel Hawthorne wrote, in *The American Note-Books,* "The ideas of people in general are not raised higher than the roofs of the houses. All their interests extend over the earth's surface in a layer of that thickness. The meeting house steeple reaches out of their sphere."

Hawthorne was careful to direct his accusation to "people in general," a category that does not and should not include writers. Any writer worthy of the title looks far beyond the meeting house steeple, into the mysteries of the unknown and the reasons for the known. He is a prober, an explorer, an interrogator, an analyst, a fact-finder, and the whole world is his business territory. Because he is all of these, he has a one-word answer to an old, old question that is put to him and other professional writers at one time or another. The question: "Where do you get your ideas?"

The all-inclusive answer: "Everywhere!"

It is true that ideas for writers *are* found Everywhere and in Everything and in practically Everyone. Some may be only seeds that, properly nurtured, can grow into book-length manuscripts. To most questioners, of course, this is not specific enough, and they want additional information. I can try to clarify the answer by telling you how some of my own books were born.

LOOK TO BOOK PEOPLE

I wrote a book called *Nature's Guardians: Your Career in Conservation* (Julian Messner, Inc., New York City, 1956, revised in 1963). When the book was first published I visited a Washington bookstore to see if copies were on sale. This is a more or less normal reaction among uninhibited authors who have not yet won a Pulitzer Prize or who admit that they like to see their names on dust jackets. Anyway, I wanted to see if my book was on the counter and prominently displayed, and if it was, I probably would loiter about for a while to see if anyone was buying a copy or even looking at one. No loitering was warranted, because the book had been ordered but not yet received by the store.

I talked with the store's book buyer, a charming lady whom I had met on a previous occasion.

"What are you working on now, Mr. Neal?" she asked.

"I'm starting another career book," I said.

"I'd like to make a suggestion."

"Fine! I'd be glad to have it."

"Well, I do wish you'd write a book about the telescope."

"The telescope?" It sounded rather dull.

"Yes. There's a real need for a reasonably priced popular book about the telescope. The only ones we have are highly technical, and we get ever so many requests from customers for a book that's readable and informative, but not so complicated."

"That's most interesting," I said, "and I'll certainly give it some thought. I do appreciate the suggestion. Thanks so much."

At that moment I was quite dubious about the value or sales possibilities of a book on the telescope, but I went home and read enough encyclopedic material to learn that some exciting and dramatic episodes were involved in the origins and development of telescopes.

After some other preliminary probing I wrote to an editor with whom I had worked telling of my conversation with the book buyer and asking her opinion of the possibilities of such a book.

"Sounds like a good idea," the editor said. "Let's do it."

So we did. The book, entitled *The Telescope,* was published (Messner) in April, 1958, and sold several thousand copies; as of 1964 it is still in print and still selling.

POINT: *Get acquainted with book buyers in retail bookstores, with the drugstore clerk who sells paperbacks, with your public librarian, and the librarians in your elementary and high schools. Let them know you're a writer seeking ideas. Ask them about subjects for which new books could fill a need or demand. What kinds of books do most customers buy or borrow? What suggestions can the booksellers and librarians offer as to types of books they'd like to see published? Is there some special need for children's books in a certain field? Most*

"book people" will be glad to give you hints or ideas for new books.

WONDER AS YOU WALK

In searching for ideas the writer must be a good observer, a good listener, an astute questioner, and a discerning reader. Whatever he sees, hears, or reads should be "programmed" into the marvelous computer that is his brain, along with the silent question: "Would this be a good subject for a book?"

So wonder as you walk. Wonder about what you see and hear. Learn to observe—not just look. Did you take a stroll yesterday, or go shopping, or go to a restaurant for lunch? If so, did you see *anything* that aroused your interest? Did you notice a bus load of handicapped children, or a peddler with a horse-drawn wagon (I'd wonder where he keeps the horse, where he has him shod, why he doesn't prefer a second-hand car)?

Do you live in a big apartment building? Did you ever wonder how many of the families that live there, under the same roof with you, know each other, and why more apartment dwellers don't try to become better acquainted with their neighbors?

Is your home in a small town? Is the town growing or shrinking, and why? Is it true that in most small towns the young people head for the big cities because jobs with good futures aren't to be found close to home—and what's the town doing about it, if anything?

Do you work in a big city? Ever look *up,* instead of straight ahead? Ever read the wording on office windows and doors? On one occasion when I visited an office building I noticed

a door with the name of a firm and the words ARTIFICIAL EYES. I wondered, "Would a magazine be interested in an article about artificial eyes?" I walked in, got the facts, wrote the piece, and sold it to *Collier's*.

Do you live in a rural area where farm auctions are frequent? Is there an auction room in your city? Why do people auction off their personal possessions? What unusual experiences have auctioneers had? Once I sought the answers to such questions and put them into another *Collier's* article.

Another time, a few years ago in New York City my attention was drawn to a small group of men and women on a street corner—I think it was Fourteenth Street and Broadway —and to the sound of music. The music wasn't of concert quality, but it was loud and brassy, and I guessed that it was coming from instruments played by members of the Salvation Army.

I hadn't seen a Salvation Army "street meeting" for a long time, and I stayed to listen and watch for a few minutes. When the music ended, a young Salvation Army officer spoke. He was a ruddy-faced, handsome youth with clear blue eyes and blond hair, and under his right ear, poking above his high uniform collar, was a purplish birthmark that reminded me of an ink blot in the famous Rorschach psychological tests.

All of the Salvation Army faces seemed to radiate a kind of sweetness and contentment, and I wondered just what the lives of these dedicated people were like. Wouldn't a probe of their motivations, their backgrounds, their philosophies, their daily tasks, make a good magazine article? At that time I was doing spare-time writing in the magazine field, because

my regular Secret Service work and responsibilities allowed little time to research many book-length ideas.

I knew as little as the next man about the Salvation Army. To me, as to most people, it meant a bass drum, a trumpet, a Christmas kettle for contributions, and a red truck that would come to one's house and pick up old furniture, clothing, or other material that might be turned to good use for the needy.

At the first opportunity I visited Salvation Army headquarters in New York and explained my mission. I wanted some preliminary information about the Army and its activities, and tentative approval for me to interview later some men and women in the ranks. I was given a sheaf of papers and pamphlets about the Army's work, and copies of its magazine *The War Cry,* and was told that I could talk with any of the Army's people whenever I was ready to do so.

After studying the printed material and talking with two officers I concluded that there was a dramatic, exciting story to tell about the Salvation Army's people at work and at home, but that its telling deserved a book rather than a magazine piece. Accordingly, I filed away the printed matter (in a folder marked "Projects for the Future") until I could spend enough time to research and write the book.

That time came after I retired from the Secret Service. I went back to the Salvation Army headquarters in New York, where I visited the Army's corps (churches) and installations in Manhattan, the Bronx, Brooklyn, and Long Island, and talked with scores of Army men and women. I prowled around the Bowery by day and by night and on one occasion sat on a platform in the Army's Bowery Corps with several former derelicts, while a Salvation Army officer told a mission

audience of bums and drunks that we on the platform had been "saved for at least three months"!

After a few weeks of daily interviews and observations I made a study of the Army's history, growth, and future plans, and finally settled down to write my book. In 1961 it was published under what I consider a good title: *The Hallelujah Army: The Salvation Army in Action* (Chilton Books).

POINT: *Had I not come upon the Salvation Army street meeting, and had I not programmed the inevitable writer's question into my skull-covered computer,* The Hallelujah Army *would never have marched into several thousand lives and homes—Hallelujah!*

HARK TO THE SMALL FRY

More than one book has been inspired by a child's question. Rose Wyler, who writes science books for children, was approached one day by a neighbor's six-year-old boy who had heard about a dog that was sent into orbit in a space capsule.

"Could you read me a book about satellites?" he asked.

"I'm sorry," she said, "but I'm afraid I don't have one that you could understand."

"Well, then—would you write one?"

That's how her book, *Exploring Space,* came into being.

Some years ago my young son and I were on a Washington playground flying a dime store kite that eventually took a dive into a tree. As we walked home we talked about what made the kite plunge and about buying another, and my boy

came up with this question: "Daddy, how did somebody first know how to make kites that would fly?"

In other words: "Where did kites come from?"

I don't even remember the answer I gave, although I think I suggested that the first kite-maker probably got his idea from watching birds in flight. The question stuck in my mind and that same night, out of a writer's curiosity, I looked up "kite" in an encyclopedia. I discovered that no one really *knew* where the very first kites originated, but that kites of many kinds had been used for serious purposes down through the ages. Later I would learn that some had been used in place of horses to pull carriages in England. Some had been used in life-saving work, some for aerial photography, some for advertising, some for Oriental kite-fights, and some for military observations. Even as late as World War II the Nazis used man-carrying kites at sea to make observations for their submarine "wolf packs."

Once again I considered doing a magazine article, this time on kites, but after several nights and weekends of research in the Library of Congress, and an interview with Paul Garber, Curator of the Air Museum of the Smithsonian Institution (himself a kite expert), I decided that the available material was sufficiently extensive and fascinating to warrant a book for children.

In the library I made notes from rare books, dug out articles in old magazines and old editions of the New York *Times,* in which I found short news items about kites. In aviation histories I read accounts of man's early attempts to fly. I wrote to the Department of Defense asking about military uses of kites. I wrote to kite manufacturers and to the National Safety Council (about rules for safe kite-flying), I

studied specimens of kites on display at the Smithsonian, and obtained some information about Oriental kites from a friend who had lived in Asiatic countries. I soon realized that kites were far more than toys, and that true stories about their serious uses could be more informative and entertaining than fiction.

When I had enough material I prepared an outline for an eight-chapter book, organized this way:

Chapter 1: THE SKY HORSE

This chapter opened with a story about four men in a carriage that was pulled by two kites instead of horses. My facts came from a rare book with an account of a 113-mile journey across England in one of these vehicles, written by a passenger. I used this episode as an opening because it was most unusual and should be an excellent interest-getter, or "hook."

Chapter 2: THE FIRST KITES

Here I traced the known history of kites, dating from centuries before Christ. To add sparkle I wrote of certain ancient legends, some dramatic, some humorous, about the kite's origin.

Chapter 3: KITES THAT FLEW PEOPLE

This chapter heading was simply a twist (instead of *People That Flew Kites*). The chapter included facts about the use of man-carrying kites, told in story form.

Chapter 4: KITES THAT HAVE HELPED US

For this chapter I condensed the well-known stories about kites flown by the Wright brothers and Benjamin Franklin, but I also told about kites that helped to build a

bridge, to measure upper-air temperatures, and to carry radio antennas aloft.

Chapter 5: EYES IN THE SKY

Early aerial photographs were made with cameras flown by kites. One of the most incredible of all true stories concerned a huge camera carried 1500 feet above the devastated city of San Francisco just after the earthquake of 1906. The photograph made by this camera was a contact print, meaning that it was the same size as the negative—4½ by 8 *feet!* To satisfy my own curiosity I located the original print in San Francisco and had a photographer make a small copy for my records.

Chapter 6: FESTIVALS AND FABLES

No book about kites would be complete unless it told of Oriental festivals and fables in which kites played a major part. Even today, kites of all shapes and sizes are flown in celebrations in countries of the Far East.

Chapter 7: LET'S MAKE A KITE

I decided that a kite book must have directions for making one or two simple kites, so I wrote instructions for making a tailless kite and a box kite. To be sure they would fly, my son and I constructed the kites according to my directions, and made test flights.

Chapter 8: GO FLY A KITE

For an appropriate finish I suggested ways in which kite-flying could be fun—using kites as motive power for swimmers, bicycle riders, skaters, etc. Here I also set out the safety rules I obtained from the National Safety Council.

On the basis of my outline and a sample chapter I got a contract from Vanguard Press, Inc., New York City, which published the book under the title *The Story of the Kite*.

POINT: *Pay attention to questions asked by children. They may spark ideas that can blaze into books for youngsters, or even for grownups.*

Listen to your own youngsters, your nieces and nephews, your neighbor's children. What are their interests? What do they have to read (in school, for example) and what would they like to read? Have the children invented new games? What kinds of new games do they wish somebody else (you, for instance!) would invent?

Out of the mouths of babes—books? Definitely!

WHAT'S THAT AGAIN?

Casual conversations with friends can be fruitful for writers, too. One night my wife and I were sitting on our porch chatting with our next door neighbors, Captain (now retired Admiral) H. L. (Joey) Ray and his wife, Ruth. Captain Ray, who knew I had written books about career opportunities for young people, asked if I were planning others. I said I was.

"Why don't you write a book about careers in naval aviation?" he asked. "We need young men in that branch, and they can make fine futures for themselves."

We talked about training, pay, promotions, and other phases of naval flying careers, and I finally wrote to a publisher to suggest military aviation as a possible career book. Their editor wisely went me one better.

"That's fine," she said, "but why not go all out? Why not cover careers in *all* phases of aviation?"

This was a real challenge, and I accepted it because it promised to be interesting and exciting, and because I knew it would fill a real need.

To get the facts for this book I visited the Air Force Academy in Colorado, the Naval Air Station in Pensacola, Florida, the Army Aviation Center in Fort Rucker, Alabama, the headquarters of a commercial airline, aircraft factories, aircraft associations and other places, to interview people doing the kinds of jobs I wanted to write about. The result: *Skyblazers: Your Career in Aviation* (Julian Messner, Inc., New York, 1958).

ANOTHER TALK, ANOTHER BOOK

The next career book I wrote also grew from a neighbor's remarks. Chris Hansen, who lived across the street from me, was Chief of the Division of Research Services at the National Institutes of Health (N.I.H.) in Bethesda, Maryland. One evening, while talking about N.I.H., Chris mentioned the urgent need for young research scientists, not only at N.I.H. but also throughout the medical research field. I asked whether he thought I could interview scientists in many research areas to learn what they did, how they did it, why they did it, and so on, and Chris said he was sure the Public Health Service would be pleased to cooperate with me in a venture that might inspire young men and women to choose medical research as a career.

The publisher I queried gave me a go-ahead on the book —and I went. I spent several weeks talking with scientists

about research in heart disease, cancer, blood diseases, dental troubles, mental illness, blindness, and other health problems, all of which I described in my book: *Disease Detectives: Your Career in Medical Research.*

After the book was published I received a long-distance telephone call from a physician in Kansas City, Missouri, who invited me to come there and deliver a one-hour lecture to members of the Kansas City Academy of Medicine.

I laughed at him. "Doctor," I said, "you have the right writer but the wrong guy! I'm not a physician. I simply wrote what I saw and heard among the real experts."

"I know that," he said. "I read about you on the book jacket. But today a lot of doctors are specialists who aren't familiar with what's being done generally in the world of medical research. I want you to come out here and tell 'em."

To make a short story swift, I accepted the invitation, lectured to members of the academy for an hour, and was honored by being made a fellow of the academy, with a handsome certificate to prove it.

Ideas, of course, aren't found only in friends, neighbors, and social gatherings. One writer chatted with a workman who came to clean a furnace in preparation for the winter season. The workman mentioned casually that he would soon be selling Christmas trees to make extra money. The remark led the writer to do a newspaper feature about the Christmas tree business. In 1961 another writer did a book about the Christmas tree.

One writer drove his car into a service station to get gasoline. He had his dog, a collie, on the back seat. The service station attendant said that his seven-year-old son had been deathly afraid of dogs until the boy's mother learned how to

rid him of his fear. How did she do that? She followed the advice of a psychologist. The writer later talked with the woman and the psychologist and wrote a magazine article suggesting how other mothers might solve similar problems.

On one occasion I was asked by a magazine editor to supply a photograph of myself. When I went to a studio to get a photograph taken, the photographer talked incessantly, evidently believing that his constant gabble would help to put me at ease. He mentioned a few interesting facts about his boss, the owner of the studio. Later I interviewed the owner and came up with a major article that appeared in *Collier's*.

So talk with (and listen to) the plumber, the postman, the mechanic, the schoolteacher, the newsboy, the barber, the waitress, and all the other people you do business with. Talk about their work, their opinions of local and national problems, their hobbies, their families. What do they think about automation, nuclear testing, space exploration, taxes, education, commodity prices, housing? Even if you get no useful ideas from such conversations, you will learn more about people and their variety of interests—cooking, gardens, child care, economics, health, crime, self-improvement, foreign affairs, government and politics, photography, ceramics, drawing and painting, woodworking, travel, history, sports, and nature. This is important to the writer, for he knows that people like to read about the things they like to talk about.

POINT: *Friends and neighbors may often have jobs which warrant a writer's exploration, or may tell of experiences which can generate book possibilities. Even when you attend social gatherings, listen to the "small talk," for it may hatch a big idea.*

SEE WRITE, THINK WRITE

Observation and curiosity are necessary tools of the non-fiction writer. Sometimes, however, the writer is so close to good ideas that he looks but doesn't see and doesn't think as a writer should.

I lived in Washington, D. C., for several years and had made several trips to the Smithsonian Institution with my children or with friends from out of town who had never seen the place. The Smithsonian is more than just a museum. It is truly a national treasure house, with such a tremendous variety of exhibits that there is something on view to interest every man, woman, or child. Besides such famous objects as the Hope diamond, the Wright Brothers' airplane, Lindbergh's *Spirit of St. Louis,* rockets and missiles, space capsules, and a lifelike elephant and whale, there are fabrics, early automobiles and locomotives, steam engines, clocks, skeletons of dinosaurs and other prehistoric creatures, fossils, meteorites, stuffed birds and animals of all varieties, military uniforms, weapons, the original "Star-Spangled Banner," and a host of other displays.

I had seen these exhibits many times, but writing about the inanimate objects resting under glass in museum cases offered little promise of exciting reading. One day I read a brief newspaper story that said certain Smithsonian scientists were fighting against time to unearth artifacts of vanished Indian tribes in the West before the sites of the Indian villages were covered by the waters of huge dams under construction in the area.

This news story induced a thought process along these lines: So the Smithsonian has its own scientists digging up

these artifacts? . . . I thought most of their stuff was presented to the museum by other people. . . . They must send representatives all over the world, probably on a variety of missions. . . . And these people must have interesting stories to tell about their personal experiences. . . .

I wrote a short query note: Would the publisher like to publish a book that would take the reader behind the scenes at the Smithsonian? Yes, he would.

At the Smithsonian, with the help of Mr. Paul Oehser, chief of its Editorial and Publications Division, and with the permission of Dr. Leonard Carmichael, its secretary and head, I arranged to interview just about all of the institution's curators or assistant curators concerning their work.

Certainly, this was a fascinating task. As in the preparation of other books, I not only learned a great deal, but also met a great many wonderful people whose experiences in the field were always interesting, often exciting and dramatic. I wrote about them and about the Smithsonian's fifty-two million objects in *Treasures by the Millions: The Story of the Smithsonian Institution.*

This book was destined to have an unusual future. In 1962 the U. S. Information Agency chose it to be produced in a paperback edition for sale and circulation exclusively in India; and in 1963 the U.S.I.A. sponsored another paperback issue printed in Burmese for use throughout Burma. Also in 1963 the Library of Congress reproduced the book in three volumes of Braille.

POINT: *Don't overlook possible book subjects on your own doorstep. The story behind something you've always taken for granted may make fascinating reading. The eight-line*

news item buried on page 10 of your morning paper could harbor a good book idea. The documentary television program you saw last night might suggest a subject for a book.

NEWS, CLUES, AND WRITERS' VIEWS

Everything you see, hear, read, and think is potentially useful to you as a writer.

Once I read a short article in a news magazine about the problems of a newspaper publisher. I thought the story of a newspaper and the people who brought it to life might make an interesting book, so I suggested the idea to a publisher. The editor countered with a proposal that newspapers be made one part of the whole story of communication among men.

Library books provided historical material about cave writing, hieroglyphics, and other early inscriptions. I wrote or talked to manufacturers of pens, pencils, ink, typewriters, cameras, radios, and communication satellites, to get information both historic and current about their products. One man I interviewed actually earned his living by making old-fashioned goose-quill pens!

My findings were set out in a book called *Communication: From Stone Age to Space Age.*

Some writers are known to clip magazine and newspaper stories on a specific subject, such as aircraft accidents, or crime, or ghosts, or trolley cars. When many clippings have been accumulated, the writers send questionnaires to individuals mentioned in the stories (or to others who may be able to furnish helpful information). Each question is followed by a blank space in which the recipient may write his

answer. The returned questionnaires and the clippings may provide enough details for a book outline and one or two sample chapters.

One writer produced a book based almost entirely on newspaper accounts of international intrigue. For "color" in describing certain foreign locales, he read guide books and travel articles written by people who had visited the places he never saw. The movie rights in the book were later sold to a Hollywood film company for a handsome figure.

I don't know what inspired Edward Gibbon to write *The History of the Decline and Fall of the Roman Empire,* but it's just possible that the idea grew from a tour of Roman ruins, or from reading a biography of Nero, or from listening to the lectures of an enthusiastic teacher of Latin.

Herman Melville's voyage aboard the whaleship *Acushnet* provided the material for *Moby Dick.* Francis Parkman kept a detailed journal of his daily activities. It was later published as *The Oregon Trail,* in which the spirit of the early West is captured and preserved.

POINT: *If you're to be a writer, read, observe, listen, and think as a writer. When you read, probe for the story behind the story. When you listen, listen for clues that may lead to salable book ideas. Somebody else's casual word may become your cashable manuscript. When you see something, see it with a writer's eye.*

Remember!

- Make friends with book buyers, public librarians, school librarians. Ask them about fields in which new books are needed.

- Wonder as you walk. Be observant. Be curious.
- Hark to the small fry. Pay attention when children ask questions or tell you about their daily activities.
- Casual conversations with friends, neighbors, repairmen, plumbers, barbers, doctors, may germinate book or article ideas.
- Don't be so close to good possibilities that you can't recognize them as book ideas. Take a second look at familiar surroundings and so-called routine activities.
- Read, listen, and see as a writer.

4

First Steps

Now let's suppose that through observation, conversation, reading, or maybe through some unaccountable and mysterious flash of inspiration, you have settled upon a subject that will make what you consider a good and salable nonfiction book. What's your next move?

How many other writers have picked the same subject for books already in print? Book publishing is a highly competitive business, and it isn't likely that a publisher will jig with joy when he receives a manuscript dealing with matters that have been covered in several recent books.

Of course there is always the possibility that your approach to a seemingly overdone subject will be new and fresh, or that it will explore some aspect that has not been *worded* to death or fully delineated by your competitors. In that event, a publisher might be willing to gamble on publishing your book—and all books are gambles to their publishers, who quite properly hope for a reasonable return on a considerable investment.

MAKE RANDOM JOTTINGS

Every writer ought to carry a pocket-size notebook or small pad so that he can write down the fleeting thought, the fresh impression, the stray idea, because any or all of these may be forever lost if the writer depends upon memory alone to preserve them. Random jottings may later be transferred to a larger, permanent notebook for future reference. Some may never be useful in a manuscript, but others might one day inspire new book ideas or segments.

What goes into such notebooks? Good examples are found in *A Writer's Notebook,* by W. Somerset Maugham (Doubleday, New York, 1949) and *The Crack-up,* by F. Scott Fitzgerald (New Directions, New York, 1945), both of which are worth reading, especially for the beginning writer.

What might go into *your* notebook? Well, what did you see or hear today that interested you? Did you learn a new word, a new fact? Did you get a new thought about that book idea or manuscript you're working on? Did you get into some controversy—and if you did, what are the opposing views?

Here are a few excerpts from my own notebooks:

The missing tooth made her smile look like a piano key-keyboard with only one black key. . . .

J. R. told me this story: A merchant seaman roomed with a couple who had three children. Another was on the way, but they didn't want it because their income was too small. The couple explained the situation to the sailor and asked him to lend them $150 to have an abortion performed. He started to give them the money, then changed his mind and offered $500 if they would have the baby. He went to sea for two years.

When he came back he called on the family. At the gate a little girl toddled toward him, laughing, her arms outstretched. "Dammit," the sailor said later, "it was just like she knew I was responsible for her being there!" . . .

Inside the Lincoln Memorial—a ragged Negro boy dances while tourists toss pennies on the floor. . . .

Dr. William Beaumont—was on scene when a man was accidentally shot with shotgun at close range. Man should have died, but Beaumont operated, saved his life. However, an opening in man's stomach refused to heal. Beaumont decided to use it for the advancement of science. Through this "window" in the stomach of an otherwise healthy man, Beaumont studied digestive processes of the human body, making discoveries that revolutionized many medical theories and beliefs. Beaumont spent most of the rest of his life keeping his man under constant observation. The man outlived the doctor. [This notebook entry, with additional details, became an important part of my book *Disease Detectives*.]

A minister's story: He and his family lived in Europe during World War II. Few people had enough food. Minister's family had stored a few loaves of bread in cellar for emergencies. They got out one loaf—the only food left to eat—and discovered it was wormy. The pastor, his wife and children, sat down at their bare table, where he offered a prayer of thanks to God for the bread. Then they turned out all the lights and ate the bread in the darkness so they couldn't see the crawling maggots. . . .

POINT: *Carry a pocket-size notebook or pad, and use it! I usually carry a small (3-by-5-inch) loose-leaf binder with ruled pages, for which I can buy fillers for a dime. If I neglect to carry it, I make random notes on envelopes or whatever other*

*paper is in my pockets, and on occasion I have bought ten-
cent notebooks in drugstores.*

KEEP RESEARCH NOTES TOGETHER

Before you begin your research, devise a method for keeping notes together. Don't combine your research notes with
those of the "daily journal" type. Some writers use loose-
leaf pages in three-ring binders, some use ruled pads, and
others make research notes on 5-by-8-inch index cards, sorted
according to chapter headings in their book outlines. Some
use typewriter paper and keep numbered pages in folders or
envelopes that can also hold newspaper clippings, pamphlets,
and other pertinent printed material—one envelope or folder
for each chapter of the book.

Me? I use both stenographic notebooks and loose-leaf fillers
and binders. I'm fortunate to be able to write shorthand,
and for a long time I wrote shorthand notes in a stenographer's notebook, then transcribed them by typewriter on
loose-leaf pages without attempting to sort them. For ready
reference I typed two or three words in the left margin opposite each paragraph or series of related paragraphs, and
then when I was ready to work on my manuscript I hunted
through the typed pages to pick out the sections I needed to
fill in my outline or chapters.

Subsequently, however, I found it easier to affix adhesive
index tabs (the "make-yourself" kind, available in any sta-
tionery store) to loose-leaf dividers, each tab bearing an ab-
breviation of a chapter heading, or the chapter number. I
then arranged my various typed pages in the appropriate
sections, so that when I began to write the book, my research

material for each chapter was all in one place. I found this to be more efficient and convenient, and I recommend it to you for trial. If you devise a system that is better for you, use it.

POINT: *Before starting research for a book (or an article), equip yourself with an ample supply of paper, and arrange to keep all of your research notes on each chapter in one place.*

SIZE UP THE COMPETITION

Your first research step is to go to the public library and check your subject in two reference works, *Books in Print* and the *Cumulative Book Index,* the latter to cover a period of at least five years. The *Cumulative Book Index* lists all English-language books of all publishers, by author's name, book title, and subject, dating from 1898. Supplements are published monthly in pamphlet form.

Look under the "subject" classification to see what's been published recently (that is, during the past five years or more) in your proposed writing area. Be sure to examine the *See also* references you'll find at the end of the subject listings. If the books in which you are interested were reviewed, you will find a brief description of their contents in the *Book Review Digest,* published annually, with monthly supplements.

In your notebook, write the full title of each pertinent book, the full name of its author, the full name of its publisher, and the year of publication. This information will be useful in at least two ways: To tell a publisher what books are available on the subject you want to write about, and to provide you with a list of references from which you may

later obtain useful information for your own writing task.

Suppose you were planning to write a book about gambling. It's probable that you would find a number of books listed under that heading, relating to racketeers, card cheats, law-enforcement problems, and various other classifications. If you wanted to write a book about gambling in general, the number in existence would probably be so great that a publisher wouldn't be interested, and you would stop right there. But—there was national interest in the legal lottery authorized by the New Hampshire legislature in 1963. Suppose you narrowed your subject down to lotteries? Chances are that the competition would be slim, the possibilities bright. Now you would search for books about the history of lotteries, legal and illegal, their advantages and evils, their successes or failures in other countries, and so on. You are not ready for *intensive* research—not yet—but you want to find out whether or not any books about lotteries have been published within the past five years, and if so, how many and what they cover.

Let's say that only two or three have appeared. In that event, you must consider the possibility that the subject *might not be worth* the writing of another book. If, however —after you have read the competing books in the field— you are convinced that there are sound reasons *your* book should have a broad appeal and an important theme or message, and if your writing is of professional caliber, your chances of interesting a publisher are pretty fair.

POINT: *Before you do a lot of research, check to see how many books have been published within the past five years, at least, that would compete with the book you want to write. If there are many, you must decide whether or not yours would be*

different enough to warrant the hard work you must do to write it. If there are few or none, proceed to plan a chapter outline and sample chapters.

READ BEFORE YOU WRITE

When you decide to go ahead, you ought to get copies of the books representing your competition and study their treatment of the subject. You may discover phases that had not occurred to you, or omissions that had, and you will probably find facts, dates, references, names, and perhaps bibliographies that could be helpful in your own research. At the very least, by reading the books you will have deepened your acquaintance with your subject, and the more you can learn about it, the more authoritative your final manuscript will be.

With this in mind it's a good idea to search at least one encyclopedia for articles relating to your project, because such articles often squeeze a great deal of useful information into a relatively short space and also may provide leads to additional research sources.

In making research notes from the encyclopedia and other books, you may want to copy pertinent excerpts exactly, or you may want to paraphrase and condense significant facts. I generally make verbatim copies of the sections I need so that later, if necessary, I can correctly quote sources for my facts.

Many large libraries have photostatic equipment or other mechanical copying devices that they use to make exact copies—which you may purchase for a fee—of printed pages of books on which copyright protection has expired. The cost is usually moderate—so much per printed page—and the

time saved that would otherwise be consumed by making notes is considerable. Inquire into this feature at your local library.

For future reference, and because on any copyrighted material you may wish to use you must obtain the permission of the copyright holder and credit the source, always make careful records of the books or other materials from which you extract information.

CAN YOU DEVOTE TIME AND TRAVEL TO RESEARCH?

At this stage, you may have to decide whether or not it is practicable for you to continue. If you have a regular daily job, for instance, and must do your research and writing in your spare time, is there enough printed material in your public library or other local places to provide the basic facts you will need? If not, can you get them elsewhere? Are there industries or organizations in or near your town where you can interview specialists about your chosen subject—and can you manage to see them during working hours? If it appears that you will have to travel to complete your research, you will have to pay for your transportation, meals, lodging, and incidentals. Can you afford the time and the expense? (Remember—some of your expenses may be deductible from your income tax.)

As for expenses, keep in mind that if you are fortunate enough to get a contract on the basis of an outline and sample chapters, your publisher will pay you an "advance against royalties," which could help to defray your costs. Such an advance might total $500 or more.

If you're a homemaker, will your household or parental

duties permit you to travel to do research, if necessary? Can you plan on conducting numerous personal interviews, morning and afternoon, and keeping your appointments? If not, wouldn't it be more practicable to choose another subject for your proposed book—one that you could research conveniently at or near your home?

If you're a senior citizen, your health or home life may be such that you cannot (or do not want to) make prolonged or even short trips by train, plane, or automobile, in order to interview people, to visit museums, or to see exhibits or manufacturing operations that should be described in your book. If so, again you might want to change your subject.

These questions and comments aren't intended to be discouraging—merely practical. We'll go into more detail about research techniques, tools, and personal interviews in a later chapter, but right now let's assume that you believe it's possible to do the necessary digging for your book and have decided to march on. On the basis of your preliminary fact-finding, you should write a chapter outline and two sample chapters to be submitted to a publisher. The outline will show how you plan to cover your subject as a whole, and the sample chapters will provide proof of your writing skill (or lack of it!).

POINT: *Take time to make sure that necessary research material is accessible to you for the book you want to write, and that you can invest whatever time and money is required to obtain it.*

Remember!

• Carry a pocket-size notebook or pad—and *use* it!
• Keep your research notes together—*not* with other notes.

- At your public library, check *Books in Print* and the *Cumulative Book Index,* for at least a five-year period, to ascertain what books would compete with the one you want to write. If there are many, consider choosing a different subject.
- Read the available books on the subject you propose to write about. Read at least one encyclopedia article on that subject.
- Research—digging for facts—takes time and may require expenses for transportation, meals, lodging, and incidentals. Be sure you can take the time and afford the expenditures, or choose another subject that can be researched more conveniently and economically.

5

Outline Your Chapters

WHY OUTLINE?

You should do enough preliminary research to enable you to write a *tentative* chapter outline for your book, and two sample chapters. I stress the word *tentative* because it is quite possible that your later intensive research will warrant changes in your original outline.

Your outline and sample chapters are, to a publisher, like swatches of cloth shown to a potential customer by a tailor. They should show enough color, texture, and quality to enable the customer (and the publisher) to decide to buy or not to buy. If the decision is negative, then the tailor needn't make the whole suit, and the writer doesn't have to write the whole book. The outline saves time and work for both editor and writer.

If the book is to be written, the outline will serve as a guide.

OUTLINE HOW?

How do you go about writing a chapter outline? What goes into it? Obviously such questions might be answered in many ways by numerous writers whose ideas and methods are entirely different from mine, but my purpose is to share my own writing experiences with you in the hope that you will find them helpful. I'll tell you how I prepared one chapter outline.

One of the most difficult—and most interesting—books I've written is *Disease Detectives*. Before I began work on this book, my knowledge of medical research was limited to articles I had read in popular magazines, and to television commercials showing aspirin tablets being dissolved in glass "stomachs."

At first I believed it would be relatively simple to write a tentative chapter outline centered around the National Institutes of Health. "Let's see, now," I thought. "There are seven distinct and separate institutes. Each is devoted to a specific research area—cancer, heart disease, and so on. I can talk with scientists at all seven, to make at least seven chapters. Then I could have one chapter on medical research history, one about nongovernmental research organizations, one about educational requirements, and one to cover any odds and ends that I miss in the others."

That's what I *thought!* What I *did* was something quite different.

After Chris Hansen answered some questions and gave me some printed material about the work of N.I.H., I read parts of two or three books about medical research, skimmed through some medical journals and two encyclopedias, and

made copious notes. From this exploration, skimpy as it was, I knew that my original approach was no good. Scientists in various medical research areas worked in several of the institutes; that is, I would find biologists, or chemists, or bacteriologists in the National Cancer Institute, the National Heart Institute, and others; and if I tried to write in detail about each institute's work and workers, I would surely be repetitive about the scientists' specialties.

In addition, I would have to include information about the pharmaceutical industry, research in hospitals, the work of many private research associations, research in the military branches, and in certain giant industrial corporations.

At least one chapter would have to deal entirely with research careers for women, not only because medical research is a good field for the girls, but also because the book should have appeal to both sexes.

What would make a better presentation than the one I conceived originally? The answer was so obvious that I would undoubtedly have thought of it in the first place *if* I had known the facts I unearthed in my preliminary research. The answer was: Center the book around the research areas themselves, not around institutes or organizations.

This was the right answer, I knew—but it created another problem. My book would have to be written in not more than 55,000 words. If I wrote about the major medical research areas, I would have to delve into biology, physiology, embryology, chemistry, biochemistry, physics and biophysics, pathology, bacteriology, mycology, entomology, parasitology, neurology, psychology, mental health, psychotherapy, genetics, sanitary engineering, virology, sensory diseases, hematology, nursing research, dental research, radiation

research, atomic medicine, pharmacology, instrumentation, medical research photography, medical art, and other fields that would interest a reader considering a career in medical research. Many technical volumes had been written on *each* of these scientific specialties—now I, in my unscientific way, proposed to squeeze them all into one readable book?

This was a real challenge, and I accepted it. Besides, it promised to be a fascinating project.

Based upon my brief talks with Chris Hansen and my preliminary reading I started work on a tentative chapter outline. How would I begin? I knew the beginning would be very important, and I thought it best to open Chapter 1 with a brief account of some modern medical research problem or discovery, such as the "atomic cocktail." This opening should capture the reader's attention and, in addition, would be told in a way to make it evident that my book was not a dry technical treatise, but that it had sparkle and life and could be read for enjoyment as well as for information.

The opening account of some modern research project could then lead smoothly into a recital of the early history and development of medicine and medical research; to the importance of medical research in all our lives today; and finally to Chapter 2, dealing with the studies of the life processes by biologists and physiologists.

In like manner, I tried to arrange the chapters so that it would be relatively easy to form a kind of natural bridge from the end of one to the beginning of the next.

In writing an outline for *your* book, should the facts be presented chronologically—or would it be better to "peg" each chapter on some current or modern undertaking as a lead-off, and then flash back to a historical analogy?

Should you tell your story with the emphasis on people or on events?

How did authors arrange their material in books similar to yours—and which of those did you find to be more effective than others? Why?

These are some of the questions that may occur to you in planning your book.

Now, here is the tentative chapter outline for *Disease Detectives,* exactly as I wrote it:

Chapter 1. THE GREEKS HAD A WORD FOR IT

Opening anecdote about the "atomic cocktail" or other very modern medical discovery; lead into importance of medical research to every human being; historical background of early medicine; recorded scientific medical system began in Greece; Greek terms still used; Hippocrates and others; dawn of modern medicine was in sixteenth century—hospitals, vaccination, inoculation, etc. Education speeds progress; new anatomical discoveries. Today's treatment of disease is based on findings of those engaged in medical research—A.M.A., N.I.H., etc.

Chapter 2. WHERE THERE'S LIFE

The biologist—studies science of life in all forms; the physiologist—studies *normal* functions of living things and their organs. What they both look for; cases showing how they work. (Note: This chapter may include some material on studies of human embryology.) Qualifications needed to become biologist, physiologist; opportunities; pay scales, etc.

Chapter 3. THE CHANGE DETECTIVES

Chemists—study characteristics of substances and the changes that take place when they combine to form other substances. Biochemists—study chemistry of living animals and plants; importance in medical research; some accomplishments; their work in industrial hygiene research. Projects under way; describe some interesting experiment from start to finish. Qualifications, opportunities, pay, etc.

Chapter 4. ALL THAT'S MATTER

The physicist—studies matter and energy *not* involving change in composition, and the action of different forms of energy on matter. Biophysicist—studies physics as applied to medicine and biology—developed high-voltage X-ray tubes to destroy cancer cells, the "radio knife," and other modern disease weapons. Some accomplishments and case histories. Qualifications, pay, etc.

Chapter 5. TROUBLE-SHOOTERS

Pathologists—study cause and nature of disease. What they do and how and why; examples; qualifications, pay, etc.

Chapter 6. THE BUG MEN

Bacteriologists—their methods and objectives; typical experiments. Mycologists—study fungi; how they work; accomplishments and aims. Entomologists—authorities on insect life; their place in medical research. Parasitologists—study science of parasites; cases, qualifications, pay, etc.

Chapter 7. THEY FIGHT THE FIDGETS

Neurologists—study the nervous system and its diseases; how they work; sample histories; qualifications, pay, etc. This work is closely allied to study of mental health.

Chapter 8. A PIECE OF MIND

Research in mental health; studies of emotional disturbances and behavior problems; psychotherapy; psychological research; effects of social and cultural factors on mental illness. Biostatistical studies important in research—why, how, and whom does a particular mental disease strike and how prevalent is it, etc. Qualifications, pay, etc.

Chapter 9. MEET GENE

Genetics (science dealing with principles of heredity and variations in animals or plants); what the geneticist does, how and why; some cases and findings; aims; qualifications and pay, etc.

Chapter 10. KEEP IT CLEAN

Research in sanitary engineering; deals with water supply systems, garbage disposal, milk pasteurization, insect and rodent control, healthful public housing, air pollution, etc. Problems, solved and unsolved. Qualifications, pay, etc.

Chapter 11. THE TINY GIANT

Virology research—study of viruses and virus diseases; case histories; accomplishments and aims. Qualifications, pay, etc.

Chapter 12. THE BIG FIVE

Research on sensory diseases—touch, sight, hearing, smell, taste. Cases, etc.

Chapter 13. LIFE IN FIVE QUARTS

Research in hematology—study of blood, etc. (There are about five quarts of blood in the normal human adult.) Work of the hematologist; cases. Qualifications, pay, etc.

Chapter 14. RESEARCH IN SKIRTS

Nursing research; other research fields for women; brief biographies of female researchers (if obtainable). Qualifications and pay, etc.

Chapter 15. AN EYE FOR A TOOTH

Dental research; examples, aims, etc. Qualifications, pay, etc.

Chapter 16. ATOMEDICS

Radiation research; atomic medicine; accomplishments and aims. Qualifications, pay, etc.

Chapter 17. BEHIND THE ℞ BRAND

Research in pharmacology—the science of drugs, their preparation, uses and effects. Pharmaceutical firms and laboratories, etc. Qualifications, pay, etc.

Chapter 18. UNCLE SAM'S HEALTH HUNTERS

The seven National Institutes of Health (Neurological Diseases and Blindness; Mental Health; Cancer; Arthritis and Metabolic Diseases; Allergy & Infectious Diseases; Heart; Dental Research). Much of their work will be described in earlier chapters, but this will show their over-all purposes, etc.; how they make research grants to many non-government institutions, universities, hospitals, etc. Public Health research.

Chapter 19. MORE TO EXPLORE

Instrumentation; science writing; medical research photography; medical art; big need for teachers; other research jobs not previously covered.

Chapter 20. WANTED: YOU!

Facts about education for research; schools, scholarships, fellowships, etc. Close with pep talk about urgent need for qualified young people in medical research fields.

Bibliography

Sources of Further Information

Index

I sent the outline to New York and my diligence was rewarded with a contract for the proposed book. Now all I had to do was get the details!

POINT: *Don't rush your preliminary research. Get enough facts to enable you to visualize your book, to write a tentative outline, and at least two sample chapters. And don't be scared off or disheartened by imagined difficulties or the apparent vastness of the subject.*

REVISING THE OUTLINE

After scores of personal interviews and many hours of reading and note-making, I decided that I had enough material to begin the writing of the book. (The subject of thorough research, including interviews, is discussed in another chapter.) First, however, I wanted to find out whether or not the chapters shown in the original outline represented a satisfactory presentation of the subject, as I now knew it, or whether some should be shifted around for a more logical, or perhaps more chronological sequence. Sometimes it is evident that the facts intended for one chapter may be more

effectively combined with those in another (or others), or that a completely new chapter is needed.

Reviewing the tentative outline for *Disease Detectives,* I decided that some changes were necessary. I cut the proposed twenty chapters to seventeen, mostly because I believed that certain medical disciplines were better combined with others than presented in chapters by themselves, and partly because I had to stay within the specified word limit.

The material about hematology (blood study), originally slated to be Chapter 13, was incorporated in Chapter 9 on genetics, because these two were closely allied. The facts about the National Institutes of Health, scheduled to fill Chapter 18, were condensed and included in Chapter 2. The decision to shorten the information about N.I.H. was based on my belief that descriptions of the actual work of scientists in the various institutes were more important for my purposes than descriptions of the institutes themselves. Moreover, by describing the aims and accomplishments of the scientists, I would be supplying the reader with detailed information about the institutes throughout the book.

I also felt that certain aspects of medical research deserved more space than sanitary engineering, so I telescoped information about the latter and did away with the proposed Chapter 10.

After studying my notes and other material dealing with medical art, medical photography, and medical writing, I chose to include these three fascinating fields in a new Chapter 15, called "Sketch, Shoot, and Scribble."

Three original chapter headings were changed. The one on neurology, "They Fight the Fidgets," I changed to "Of All The Nerve," and the one called "The Bug Men" became

"The Mold and Bug Men"; the reason being, in both instances, that the revised headings were more descriptive of the chapter content.

The original final chapter, Chapter 20, I changed from "Wanted: You!" to "Tools for Tomorrow," because I could logically combine facts about new scientific discoveries and inventions with promises of new outlooks and challenging futures for young people in the world of medical research, and the new chapter title was more fitting than the original.

Chapter 12, outlined to deal with sensory diseases, was eliminated, but significant facts about such ailments were dropped into appropriate places in other chapters.

Here, then, on the following page is the table of contents as it actually appeared in the published book *Disease Detectives*.

In this instance I felt that the changes in my original outline were not of such major importance that I should consult the publisher about them. But if they had represented an entirely new or different approach to the subject, as compared with my original presentation, then it would have been wise (and courteous) to show the revision to the publisher, who might offer helpful comments or suggestions, or raise questions that could lead to still more changes.

POINT: *Be prepared to revise your original outline when you've completed your research. You will have acquired a host of new facts and a deeper understanding of your subject, and these may warrant an approach quite unlike the one with which you started. If there are major and significant differences between the two outlines, discuss the final version with the publisher.*

CONTENTS

Remember!

- Your preliminary research should provide you with enough facts to write a *tentative* chapter outline and at least two sample chapters.
- There are no hard and fast rules about writing chapter outlines. Each presentation must be governed by the facts at hand and by the author's choice and arrangement of those facts.
- When your research is completed, you may have to revise your tentative outline. Can you improve your original presentation, your arrangement of chapters? Should any chapters be shortened or lengthened or eliminated? Should new ones be added? Give your original outline a long, hard look.
- If you make major changes, write or talk to the publisher about them.

6

The Sample Chapters

When you are satisfied that you have completed your best possible outline, select a chapter about which you know the most and write a complete version of that chapter. Two chapters are preferable, and most publishers require *at least* two, along with the outline, from hitherto unpublished writers.

There's no rule that says your sample chapters must be the first two indicated in your outline, but it's obvious that Chapters 1 and 2 will help a publisher to evaluate the continuity and organization of the rest of the outline, so it is usually best to write the first two chapters as your samples.

I have found that in most instances Chapter 1 is easier to write than those that follow, because it is primarily an introduction and may not require the extensive research that must precede the writing of the others. It may well be that you cannot write the two sample chapters without doing consid-

65

erable research to get the facts you need. In that event, do the research!

Don't try to fake your facts, and don't bloat your sample chapters with superfluous words and sentences just to take up space, because an editor can spot such chicanery quicker than you can say, "Rejection slips sting worse than whips!"

You may want to show your sample chapters to some competent critic before sending them out. What's a "competent" critic? Perhaps another writer, a teacher of English, or just a well-educated friend who can raise questions about statements he doesn't understand, or about word usage, or other aspects of your writing. If you do go to a friend you must select him carefully. It is difficult for a friend, and *impossible* for a member of your family, to be objective. If you feel that your critic's comments or suggestions warrant changes in your manuscript, by all means make the changes; but if you disagree and are convinced that changes are not needed, don't make them. *You* are the author.

POINT: *The sample chapters that accompany your outline should represent the very best writing you can produce, for they are your spokesman in the editorial offices. They are your commercial, your sales pitch, your opening bid for a book contract. If your writing is poor, so are your chances to interest a publisher.*

OPENINGS

How do you begin a chapter? During workshop sessions I've conducted at writers' conferences, class members have asked such questions as, "Can I begin an article with a story about a man who went crazy trying to invent a new kind of

ketchup bottle?" Or, "Is it permissible to start a book about my great-grandmother by telling how my great-grandfather made moonshine in South Carolina?"

The key words in these questions are *"Can I"* and *"Is it permissible."* The only answer has to be "You certainly can" or "Of course it is." As the author of a book, a magazine article, a short story, a poem, an essay, or whatever, you can write anything you please. You're not bound by any laws. Your manuscript is yours alone, and you may put into it what you will. In the first place, you don't want to imitate some other writer. Secondly, your opening, your whole manuscript, written as *you* want it, may be far superior in style, pace, and magnetic attraction to that of any of your contemporaries.

Always keep in mind, however, that *you must attract and hold the attention of your reader*—a person who is a stranger to you and who figuratively may be daring you to make him want to read your book.

I'll tell you about some of the beginnings I've used, and I offer them merely as thought-provokers, not with any intention of suggesting that you should adopt similar techniques. If they are helpful to you, my purpose will have been served.

THE ANECDOTE

A brief story involving people in action is what I call an anecdotal opening. According to the Funk & Wagnalls *Standard College Dictionary,* an anecdote is "a short narrative of an interesting or entertaining nature." Chapter 1 of *Treas-*

ures by the Millions: The Story of the Smithsonian Institution has this anecdotal opening:

Two white men stepped out of a small boat on the beach at Gonâve Island, off the mainland of Haiti, and hiked inland to the Village of the Voodoo Queen.

One was Dr. Alexander Wetmore, a renowned ornithologist; the other, Mr. Watson Perrygo, an expert taxidermist. They were from the Smithsonian Institution in Washington, D. C., and were on the island to collect various kinds of birds for their museum.

Entering the village, they were watched by scores of hostile natives, some of whom went into their thatched huts and came out with spears. The explorers halted and Dr. Wetmore spoke to a tall, muscular man who stood before a hut with his arms folded.

"We come to see your Queen," Dr. Wetmore said in French.

The native shook his head. "The Queen is not here."

Slowly the other residents of the village began to encircle the white men.

"We come to hunt birds," Dr. Wetmore said. "We only want to make our headquarters in your village for a few days."

The tall man turned to his companions and held a whispered conversation, then spoke again. "You pay one thousand dollars each day?"

"A thousand dollars? That's ridiculous," Perrygo said.

"That is what you pay to stay," the native answered.

In English, Dr. Wetmore said, "It's their way of saying we're not welcome."

"So what do we do now?" Perrygo asked.

Dr. Wetmore attempted to bargain with the spokesman without success. As they were about to depart he reached into his knapsack and brought out a small flashlight. He stuck the

bulb end in his mouth, pushed the button, and watched the natives' startled reaction as his cheeks glowed red. Then he released the button and removed the light from his mouth, whispering to Perrygo, "Now *you* do something to surprise them. Go on—do anything!"

Perrygo did the only unusual thing he could think of at the moment. He walked on his hands! The Haitians had never seen such a performance, and when Perrygo regained his feet they were so impressed by the magic light and the man who walked upside down that they broke into smiles and insisted that the explorers stay in the village free of charge. A family was evicted from its hut and the white men were ushered into their new home. . . .

I chose this kind of opening because much of the balance of the book was to consist of personal accounts of other Smithsonian scientists in the field. The opening anecdote had some drama, some humor, and helped to set the stage for the acts to follow. It also led smoothly into a description of the Smithsonian, its history and purposes.

THE DECLARATION

Another book, *Communication: From Stone Age to Space Age,* begins with what we might call a declaratory opening— one which rather quickly declares plainly what the whole book is about. The first chapter is headed "Grunts, Giggles, and Talking Hands," and it opens this way:

The Bible says that the first words ever spoken by a human being were names given to "all cattle, and to the fowl of the air, and to every beast of the field" by Adam, the first man. And the first quoted words of the first man, spoken just after

God had created Eve, the first woman, were: *This is now bone of my bones, and flesh of my flesh; she shall be called Woman, because she was taken out of Man* (Genesis 2:23).

Some scientists do not agree with the Bible statement, *And the Lord God formed man of the dust of the ground and breathed into his nostrils the breath of life; and man became a living soul.* Many are convinced that man developed, instead, from some lower form of life, such as the anthropoid apes, and that his transformation from beast to human began about a million years ago.

It isn't our purpose to argue about the evolution of man, as such. This book is about another kind of evolution—the evolution of speech and of writing and of other forms of communication that have, in our own time, brought all nations, all peoples, closer to one another, squeezing the world from a huge globe down to a big "O."

THE SURPRISE

This kind of opening might also be called the "eyebrow raiser." Most readers enjoy being surprised, and many writers make successful use of odd and unusual facts to capture attention quickly. In doing research for *Engineers Unlimited: Your Career in Engineering,* I found some fascinating information about the engineering genius of some of nature's creatures, and I used it to open Chapter 1 in this fashion:

The world's first engineers had no hands, could not talk, and worked entirely by instinct, using only such building materials as nature provided. Their methods have not changed.

The honey bee, for example, uses her tongue as a pump to transfer nectar from flowers into her stomach, then manufactures the nectar into honey and deposits this sweet liquid in

a perfectly engineered six-sided wax cell in a honeycomb built by her and her industrious companions.

In a beehive the heat of the insects' bodies sometimes makes their home too hot, in which case certain bees are put to work fanning their wings to drive out the hot air—a living air conditioner!

Some species of bees excavate tunnels and live underground, while others carve holes in trees to make their homes.

A buzzin' cousin of the bee is the wasp, the first engineer to manufacture paper. It chews wood into a wet pulp, forms the pulp into a thin sheet and lets it dry, then uses the paper to build a nest. The pages of this book were made by man and machine, but the basic method was the same as that used by the wasp.

Some spiders build what we call webs, but these are really suspension bridges as carefully engineered as those men make of steel.

Many birds and animals construct nests that are engineering masterpieces. The East Indian swift actually spits out a neat hemispherical home, using saliva that dries like clay. Real clay is used for nesting by the red ovenbird of South America, and her finished house is often a foot or more in diameter.

The beaver is the best dam builder in nature's world.

From this opening I led into an account of some unusual engineering accomplishments by humans, and into a history of engineering techniques and devices.

THE NEWS-PEG

In 1959, when I was writing *Disease Detectives,* there was wide public interest in the exploration of outer space. No

astronaut had yet been hurled into orbit around the earth, but such an adventure was in the planning stage. I decided to "peg" the opening of this book on the newsworthy space research then in progress. Chapter 1 begins like this:

A tribe of South American Indians, living closer to outer space than any other people, may help the first human space traveler to survive.

The Indians live in the small mining town of Morococha in the Andes Mountains of Peru, nearly three miles high. At this altitude the pressure of the atmosphere is only about one-half of the sea-level pressure, and if you or I were to be plunked down on the Main Street of Morococha we would probably feel lightheaded, maybe a little dizzy or dreamy, and if we did any physical exercise we would breathe much faster than at lower altitudes—all because of a shortage of oxygen in the air.

The people of Morococha, who were born and raised in this cloudland, have been equipped by nature to live and work as normally as any other humans. They have great bulging chests which cover very large lungs that suck in huge quantities of the rarefied air, and their blood is patterned to get the fullest benefit of every scrap of oxygen. They do heavy physical work without huffing or puffing, and they go in for rough and fast sports such as soccer, just as Americans do for football or hockey.

Morococha became a kind of laboratory in 1957, when the United States Air Force, deeply interested in space medicine, sought answers to two questions:

Could an average man, living at sea level, adjust himself to the same kind of rarefied air breathed by the natives of Morococha; and could he make this adjustment in a few weeks, when it has taken the Indians centuries?

If a man could make the adjustment, and if he were then hurled into outer space in a rocket ship and accidentally

lost his oxygen supply, would his adjustment help him to stay alive?

I then told how the Air Force, with its own volunteers, made studies to find answers to these questions. The account of this Air Force research project was followed by this paragraph:

Through research such as this, scientists are learning more and more about *inner* space—the world's most amazing mechanism, the human body. They will freely admit that there are still many secrets of life which they hope to uncover, but they will also allow that great discoveries about life and death have been made since blood first began to flow in the veins of man.

This was a transition paragraph, providing a bridge to a recital of the "magic, superstition, and general hocus-pocus" used by physicians and healers in the ancient world—a prologue to the modern methods and discoveries in medical science described in the rest of the book.

THE HISTORIC

In *Pathfinders, U.S.A.,* I plunged headlong into history for my opening, for reasons which will be obvious when you read it:

A swashbuckling American soldier named John Charles Frémont, with a handful of picked men, braved the unknown wilderness of the American West to explore the rugged Rocky Mountains in 1842. Frémont fixed the position of the South Pass in the Rockies and then, dwarfed by the majestic peaks around him, he made a careful study of the astronomy, the geography, the botany, the geology, and the meteorology of

that entire region. Armed with his findings, he made recommendations for the sites of a line of forts, which were later built to protect our Westward expansion.

In 1836 Frémont, at 23, was a civil engineer, making a survey of the Cherokee Indian lands in the South. Later he explored the frontiers in Minnesota, the Dakotas, Nebraska. In 1838, he became a second lieutenant in the U. S. Topographical Corps, mapping strange new territory.

His adventurous life and his eagerness to push toward new horizons won him the popular nickname, "The Pathfinder."

The jobs Frémont did were exciting, worthwhile, and varied —and so are those you will read about in the pages ahead, for many are jobs of the same kind. This book is about the challenging careers to be found by young people in certain aspects of five stimulating fields: Roadbuilding, Shipping, Civil Aviation, Coastal and Land Surveying, and Meteorology (Weather).

The people who do these jobs are modern pathfinders, just as Frémont was in his day, and our title, *Pathfinders, U.S.A.*, seems to sum up their stories and objectives better than any other.

The terms I have used to describe the various kinds of beginnings—*Anecdote, Declaration, Surprise, News-Peg, Historic*—are simply words that seemed to fit. Others might be more descriptive, more appropriate. The headings are immaterial. What matters is that there are as many ways to write an opening paragraph or chapter as there are writers. Your way may be better than any yet written.

POINT: *Don't ask, "Can I write it this way?" You can, if you want to. You are the master of your own creation. Your words are puppets, and you are the puppeteer. Write in*

whatever way you believe is most forceful, most effective, most likely to arouse and hold the attention of the readers with whom you hope to communicate.

Remember!

- Your outline and sample chapters are your sales representatives. Write them with care. If competent criticism is available to you, consider seeking it before sending out your material.
- There are as many ways of beginning a book as there are books or writers. The opening should have one primary aim—to attract and hold a reader's attention.
- Don't worry if your chapter opening is unlike any you've ever seen before, and don't ask yourself if such an opening is "permissible." You're the author. Write in what you consider the most effective way.

7

Selecting a Publisher

Now that your book outline and sample chapters are ready, it's time to put them to work. How? Send them to a publisher! That's dandy—but what publisher? One who sells the kind of book you've outlined.

If your book deals with religion or theology, you wouldn't send it to a company that publishes westerns, mysteries, and sexy romances. If it's about the care and breeding of monsters from other worlds, a publisher who specializes in books on the fine arts might be personally interested in your feeding formulas but never in producing your book.

There are several ways in which you can learn publishers' specialties. So-called "market lists" are found in writers' magazines, or the *Writer's Market (Writer's Digest,* 22 East 12th Street, Cincinnati 10, Ohio, $5.95), or the *Writer's Handbook (The Writer,* 8 Arlington Street, Boston 16, Massachusetts, $6.95). One excellent reference work is the *Literary*

Market Place (R. R. Bowker Company, 1180 Avenue of the Americas, New York 36, New York), which lists not only book publishers, but also literary agents, clipping bureaus, and other services of interest to writers. New editions of all three books are published yearly.

Market listings are necessarily brief and general. Typical examples read something like this:

FUNK & WAGNALLS CO., INC.
360 Lexington Ave., New York 17
Fiction, general nonfiction, juveniles, dictionaries, reference, mail order.

BARNES & NOBLE, INC.
105 Fifth Ave., New York 3
Educational & scholarly paperback & hardbound originals & reprints.

Because of the general tone of such listings, it is wise to make a further market study. In the *Cumulative Book Index* or the annual listing *Subject Guide to Books in Print* you can easily find classifications of books similar to your own and see who published them.

An inspection of library books on subjects allied to yours will show which publishers are interested in those subjects, and your public librarian may be able to make helpful suggestions about a publisher for your book.

Bookstore managers have frequent visits from publishers' salesmen and are well-informed about various book categories and who publishes what.

In magazines such as *Atlantic Monthly, Harper's, The New Yorker, Saturday Review, Publishers' Weekly,* and in newspaper supplements such as the New York *Times Book Review,* you will find publishers' advertisements describing new books.

Inexpensive paperback originals are becoming increasingly in demand by publishers, and in your search for a firm to publish your book you should consider those which issue

paperbacks, as well as those producing only hard cover editions.

If you have some specific publisher in mind, you can get his address from his ads, from the *Cumulative Book Index* or the *Literary Market Place,* the market lists, or from your bookstore. Write for a copy of his trade list or catalogue, which will set out the titles and descriptions of his firm's books. From these you can determine whether or not yours might warrant his consideration.

POINT: *Send your outline and sample chapters only to firms that publish books on subjects similar to yours.*

BIG HOUSE OR SMALL HOUSE?

Some authors believe that it is to their advantage to approach a big publishing house rather than a small one, and perhaps it is. The big house may put out several hundred new books each year, as compared to perhaps ten or twelve by a small firm, so the chances for publication seem greater. Looking at the other side of the page, however, it is likely that the big publisher receives a flood of manuscripts, the small publisher only a trickle; and to the author this means that his competition is in proportion to these submissions. Bear in mind, though, that because of his limited output, the small publisher must be more selective.

There is also the possibility that a big publisher will advertise a new book along with a host of other new books, with no one work getting any special promotion, while a smaller company with only a few new titles may place individual advertising emphasis on each one. While it is generally conceded that advertising alone will not get a book to the top of

the best-seller list, properly placed ads can lend substantial impetus to a book that has already started to move.

Of course if you have a literary agent, your outline and chapters would be sent to him or her, and the agent would choose and approach the likely markets. The role of the literary agent is discussed later in this book.

POINT: *As the author, you must weigh the advantages of working with a big publishing house against those of working with a small one. If publishers from one group don't want your book, those from the other might. If it's your first book, getting it published by a reputable firm is more important than the firm's size.*

DEAR SIR: ENCLOSED FIND BOOK IDEA

You're now going to mail your sample chapters and outline to the publisher of your choice, accompanied by a letter which is your "sales pitch." Find out the name of the editor in chief, or of any other editor and address him by name. If you expect an editor to take the time to read your material, surely he can expect you to take the time to find out his name. Here is a sample of the kind of information you should provide:

Dear Mr. ——:

Enclosed are sample chapters and a tentative outline for a book I propose to write concerning career opportunities for young men and women in medical research.

Preliminary talks with medical research scientists have revealed that the need for qualified people in this field is desperate, and that too little is being done to make young men and women aware of this need.

I have established that six books dealing with careers in or related to medical research have been published during the past ten years, and only one of these appeared within the last five years. A list of the books is attached for your information. [Your list will include title, author, publisher, year, and price.]

In examining these books I have found that they are written in rather general terms, one covering only biology and physiology, and one stressing psychology and psychiatry. Those dealing broadly with medical research were published so long ago that much of their information is obsolete, especially in terms of the latest research developments and devices.

I have been assured that I may personally interview qualified scientists in practically all medical research disciplines at the National Institutes of Health in Bethesda, Maryland, to get first-hand information about the work they do and how they do it. I am not a scientist, but I propose to make my book authoritative by actual quotations from the specialists themselves, and by reporting my own observations in the laboratories and offices I visit.

This approach, although directed toward potential candidates for medical research careers, should have an appeal for readers of all ages. Most people are intensely interested in health and medical science, and I propose to go behind the scenes to show the kinds of research now in progress to fight cancer, heart disease, mental illness, and other serious human ailments.

My outline is tentative because I have not as yet begun intensive research, and because I realize that if you are interested in publishing my book you may have some constructive suggestions about modifying, enlarging, or otherwise revising the presentation. Also, when my research has been completed I may find that the tentative outline can be improved by some

reorganization and revision, based on material I do not now have.

As for my background, I am fifty-six years old, married, a retired government employee, and I have had a number of articles and short stories published in several national magazines. [If you have never been published, say so.]

I would be pleased to discuss my book idea with you at some mutually convenient time and place.

A word of warning: Never, never, never send copies of your outline and sample chapters to more than one publisher at a time. If you do, and if you get two or three acceptances, you will find yourself in a most awkward situation, and one which may be prejudicial to you in any future editorial overtures or negotiations.

POINT: *Your letter transmitting your sample chapters and outline to a publisher should set out all conceivable reasons why you believe your book would have reader appeal.* Caution: *Query only one publisher at a time, to avoid embarrassment and possible future difficulty.*

THE SIMPLE QUERY

Under certain circumstances you may prefer to delay the writing of sample chapters until you receive some indication of a publisher's interest in your book idea. For example, it may be that authorities from whom you must obtain facts essential to the writing of sample chapters would not want to agree to interviews, with the resultant loss of time from their work, if it appeared that you were depriving them of this time on a purely speculative project. During some of my own research, even when I had a signed contract for a book, I was

told by experts I interviewed that because of their work they must limit our discussion time.

If there are logical reasons why you cannot submit sample chapters, it should still be possible for you to organize some kind of *tentative* outline, based on library research, that will convey an idea of the ultimate content of your book. You can also enclose your list of the books in print that might compete with yours. You might then write a query letter to a publisher, along these lines:

Dear Mr. ——:

Enclosed is a tentative outline for a book I want to write about careers in medical research.

[Set out the pertinent information as illustrated in the previous sample letter.]

[Give the reasons you have not written sample chapters and explain that you will be glad to submit samples if the publisher is interested in your idea.]

It is possible, of course, that your book will not require personal interviews. It may, for example, be historical in nature, necessitating mostly library research. In that event, you should be able to write sample chapters. But if you prefer, you might first approach the publisher with a letter outlining your idea and asking if he would be interested in seeing sample chapters.

POINT: *Although it is preferable to have an outline and sample chapters before you approach a publisher, an explanatory letter might, under certain circumstances, be sufficient to determine whether or not he has any interest in the subject.*

When your material arrives in the publisher's office, it is unlikely that the editorial staff will shout with glee, "Eureka! We have found it!" If the firm is a big one with many employees, your manuscript will go to one of several editorial assistants whose job it is to read what you (and other struggling writers) have written, and decide whether it has enough merit to be referred to a higher echelon.

If this assistant editor has ten or fifteen other submissions in his incoming mail basket, he will put yours on the bottom of the stack, to be reached in its proper turn. If you've sent your material to a small publishing house, there may be only one or two editors to read and edit manuscripts and to carry on the necessary correspondence. There is also the possibility that the person who is to read your work may be on vacation, or ill, or out of the city on business, or engaged in some other task that has priority.

For reasons such as these, it is conceivable that you will not receive a decision from the publisher for several weeks, except perhaps for a postcard acknowledging receipt of your letter. Therefore, don't be too impatient. If, within four to six weeks, you have had no word from the publisher, write him a letter worded somewhat as follows:

Dear Mr. ——:

With a letter dated January 16 I sent you an outline and two sample chapters of a proposed book about career opportunities in medical research. More than a month has since elapsed, and I am wondering whether you have had a chance to read my material, and if not, whether you would be good enough to tell me when I may expect your decision.

I have made tentative arrangements to interview a number of specialists to get material for the book, and I am anxious to begin my research before it becomes necessary to renew my original requests for their cooperation.

This follow-up may not be necessary, since the publisher may write to you within a week or two after he receives your manuscript. He may respond in one of several ways:

- He may express an interest in your project and suggest that if you care to complete the book he will be glad to consider the finished manuscript.
- He may say that he would prefer to see three or four more completed chapters before making a final decision; and he may add that his statement is not to be construed as an agreement of any kind.
- He may ask you to come to his office to discuss the book.
- He may offer you a contract. (Contracts are discussed in a later chapter.)
- He may return your material with a brief letter saying that he is sorry, but that he cannot consider it for publication at this time; or he may return it with a printed rejection slip.

If he rejects it, don't be discouraged even a smidgin. Some of the most successful books in publishing history were rejected by a dozen or more publishers before they finally found acceptance. So what do you do? You send your outline and samples, with another letter, to another publisher— and another and another—until you are *sure* you have exhausted every possibility; and then start down the list again, for editors and policies and times change and publishers' needs vary, but if you have faith in your own work (as you

must), you should be confident that somewhere there is a publisher who will share that faith.

If you are fortunate enough to receive professional criticism from any editor, you would do well to consider it carefully, and if you feel it is valid, amend your material accordingly. Especially, if you receive the same suggestion from more than one editor, it is likely that your material is lacking in this particular respect. Busy editors can rarely afford the time to criticize unsolicited material unless they feel it has some publishing possibilities.

After each rejection, then, you would be wise to reread your manuscript to see whether it can be revised to advantage.

POINT: *There are many reasons why a publisher may delay a decision about your manuscript. He may choose one of several possible responses—but if he rejects your work, don't be discouraged. Other publishers may be seeking exactly the kind of book you want to write. Have faith in your own work.*

Remember!

- Check to see which firms publish books in the category of your book idea. Don't waste your time and postage, or an editor's time, by sending your outline and sample chapters to houses that do not publish in your field.
- Your outline and sample chapters should be accompanied by a letter addressed to some particular editor setting out every reason why you believe your book would have wide reader appeal.

- If there are good reasons why you can't submit sample chapters, write a *tentative* outline and a letter stating why your book is worth publishing.
- Never send your query to more than one publisher at a time.
- Don't be discouraged by rejections. Some of the most famous authors have been turned down more than once.
- Your submission—of material that you want back—should be accompanied by a self-addressed stamped envelope.

8

Paperwork Research

As I've told you, *Disease Detectives* was a difficult project for me (as most of my books have been) because I had to start from scratch in unknown territory. At the outset I knew nothing whatever about medical research, and by the time my first outline was prepared I knew only a little. After I signed my contract, I had to acquire more than enough knowledge to fulfill the promise of my chapter outline—a realization that has sometimes led to a passing thought like, "Why don't I keep my big trapwriter shut?"

In all honesty, though, I can say that I have enjoyed every writing project I have undertaken. Each presents new problems, new challenges, provides new acquaintanceships, and adds immeasurably to my growing fund of knowledge. This was certainly true of *Disease Detectives.*

I began to ferret out information from a variety of sources. Since I couldn't afford to travel extensively, I went to the

public library and searched more scientific and medical journals for possible leads. Magazine advertisements of chemical
and pharmaceutical companies furnished helpful information such as their respective specialties and names and addresses of additional sources. Some articles mentioned scientific organizations of which I had never heard, and whose
names (and addresses, if published) went into my notebook.
The contents of the journals themselves provided valuable
bases for later interviews, although their scientific language
sometimes befuddled my unscientific mind.

MAIL-ORDER HELP

On the basis of such searches, I wrote to certain groups:
the American Medical Association, the American Association
for the Advancement of Science, the American Chemical
Society, the American Institute of Biological Sciences, and
perhaps a score of other associations, societies, and institutes.
I also wrote to a number of drug manufacturers, chemical
companies, life insurance companies, medical schools, government agencies such as the Scientific Manpower Commission, the Surgeon General's office, and the Atomic Energy
Commission.

What did I say in my letters? Well, here's a copy of one
addressed to a pharmaceutical company:

Dear Sirs:

I understand that your company has published a booklet
called *Your Career Opportunities in Pharmacy*. I am now
gathering material for a book about career opportunities in
medical research, and since a part of this book will deal with
careers in pharmaceutical research, I am wondering if you

would be kind enough to send me a copy of your booklet?

If you have any other material concerning the work of your company in pharmaceutical research, or if you have any comments or advice you would like to offer to young people who are considering this field, I would be glad to have them for possible use in my book.

I shall be most grateful for whatever assistance you can give me.

As an example of the kind of responses my letters received, I quote the reply made by this same pharmaceutical firm:

Dear Mr. Neal:

Complying with your request, I am enclosing a copy of *Your Career Opportunities in Pharmacy,* also copies of *Our Smallest Servants* (the story of fermentation) and *Men, Molds and Molecules.*

Reprints and tearsheets of several articles by our scientific personnel also may be useful. On the chance that you have not seen the Health News Institute booklet, *Facts About Pharmacy and Pharmaceuticals,* I am also enclosing a copy of that.

If your work takes you to New York, you are invited to look through our Public Relations Reference Library of books and periodical clips. The collection, accumulated in recent years, is fairly extensive.

We also have an archive of historic photographs depicting the history and development of medicine, and a number of pictures portraying the work of the pharmacist. Prints could be made for your use.

In any case, when your new book is published next year, I know we will want at least one copy for our library.

Please feel free to write again or call any time you think we can assist you in your research.

Without exception, every one of my mail inquiries was productive. The sources that could provide no information bearing directly on medical research suggested others to whom I might write.

Useful information is sometimes available from a source you might not ordinarily consider—the Congress of the United States. Here is the text of a letter I sent to Senator Lister Hill of Alabama, which is self-explanatory:

Dear Senator Hill:

I am gathering material for a career book which will describe opportunities for young men and women in medical research, to be published by Julian Messner, Inc., New York City, in 1959.

In a feature story in the New York *Times* for September 14, 1958, I read about a proposal for an international health-research program that you introduced in Congress, designed to "encourage and support research and the exchange of information on research, the training of research personnel, and the improvement of research facilities throughout the world."

The *Times* article also mentions a $300,000 grant made by the United States to the World Health Organization for a preliminary study "to lay the groundwork for medical research on an international basis."

I would appreciate having a copy of your bill, together with any other printed material you may have which would be pertinent to my project. I would also welcome any comment you might care to make (for possible quotation in the book) about the importance of medical research as a career for qualified young people.

Senator Hill sent me a gracious reply and a copy of the

resolution I asked for, part of which is quoted in the published book.

In this instance, as you noted, I read about Senator Hill's proposal in the New York *Times.* You might not find a similar lead for the subject on which you want to work, but there's no reason why you shouldn't write to your own representatives or senators, explaining your project and asking them if there is any recent or pending legislation relating to it. If so, say that you would appreciate having copies of the bills, committee reports, or records of public hearings. If hearings have been held, the printed testimony of witnesses may be a gold mine of helpful facts which you can use.

POINT: *You can accomplish a great deal by writing letters to manufacturers, congressmen, and others, asking for printed matter relating to your book idea, or listing questions to be answered by experts. All of my written inquiries were productive, but even if only half of them brought results, the time spent in their preparation would have been well worth while.*

JOIN FORCES WITH MUSEUMS AND LIBRARIES

Two marvelous sources of information are the Smithsonian Institution and the National Archives, both in Washington, D. C. The Smithsonian can supply information in almost every field of science and history. The National Archives maintains records of federal government agencies, many dating back a century or more, and will make microfilm copies available for research at a moderate cost. If you are searching for scientific or historical material, don't overlook these two agencies.

Remember, too, that museums in or near the city where you live can often be helpful to you. Many of them sell publications on a variety of subjects, written by curators or other members of museum staffs. The curators themselves are always glad to answer intelligent questions about the fields in which they specialize.

One of the most helpful people in any writing project is your public librarian. He, or more often she, is a walking, talking repository of information neatly catalogued and ready to be dispensed for the asking. Too few people, including many writers, appreciate the extent of assistance a librarian can offer, and too many hesitate to avail themselves of her free services. Not only does she know what books are on her shelves, but also she has read a great many of them and can be selective in her recommendations. In addition to books, she often maintains a "vertical file" (meaning a filing cabinet!) packed with all sorts of leaflets, pamphlets, booklets, and other publications on a wide range of subjects.

In many states, if not all, local librarians can send requests to the public library in the state capitals for books that are not available locally. For example, I do some research in the county library in Culpeper, Virginia, near my home. Miss Crimora Waite, the very helpful librarian there, has sent requests for books to the library in Richmond, and I get them within a week. If I do not know the titles and authors of books dealing with the subject I'm writing about, Miss Waite simply asks for several books relating to that subject, and the librarian makes a representative selection.

Libraries in universities and colleges may also be helpful. In addition to popular books and textbooks, they have copies of theses written by students doing graduate work, and it is

always possible that a thesis has been written on the very subject on which you are working.

POINT: *Don't overlook museums and historical societies in or near the town where you live (or the Smithsonian Institution or the National Archives both in Washington, D. C.) as sources of research material.*

Don't sell short your local librarian as a partner in your book project. She can often find or refer you to sources you'd never think of.

A FEW REFERENCE WORKS YOU SHOULD KNOW ABOUT

Many libraries have a wealth of valuable reference works in addition to the well-knowns such as the *Funk & Wagnalls Encyclopedia,* the *Encyclopaedia Britannica,* the *Encyclopedia Americana,* the *World Book Encyclopedia* and *Collier's Encyclopedia.* Here are a few that every writer should know about: *The Catholic Encyclopedia* (for Roman Catholic doctrines, history, etc.); *The Jewish Encyclopedia* (for Jewish history, religion, customs); *Encyclopedia of the Social Sciences* (for information on anthropology, ethics, economics, politics, law, psychology, and various social problems); *Van Nostrand's Scientific Encyclopedia* (providing facts about a wide variety of basic and applied scientific research in language understandable to the average reader); *Grove's Dictionary of Music and Musicians* (for almost anything you want to know about musical instruments, history, terminology, composers, and musicians). Many other specialized encyclopedias and invaluable information sources are listed in the *Guide to Reference Books.* And *Subject Guide*

to Reference Books will tell you what's available according to subject.

Don't overlook dictionaries, such as the *Funk & Wagnalls Standard College Dictionary, Webster's, Oxford,* all of which carry a great deal of information in addition to word definitions.

The *World Almanac* and *Information Please Almanac* offer thousands of facts and statistics for quick reference. Sometimes *old* issues of these and other reference works are helpful.

Facts on File is a thumbnail digest of daily newsworthy events, published on punched pages and kept in loose-leaf binders. Here you can get all the significant news on national and international affairs, politics, entertainment, sports, business, and other subjects, in capsule form.

If you want to check on speeches, essays, costumes, poems, and myriad other classifications, there are many published indexes showing where you may find what you seek. One of the most useful of these is the *Essay and General Literature Index,* by Minnie E. Sears and Marion Shaw, which tells where to find various essays and books on a host of subjects. There is a *Speech Index* by Roberta B. Sutton, a *Costume Index* by Isabel Monro and D. E. Cook, an *A.L.A. Index to General Literature* (covering biographical sketches, monographs, essays, and various literary and historical societies), an *Index to Short Stories,* an *Index to Plays,* even a *Song Index.*

Two more good tools for writers are books called *How and Where to Look It Up* (McGraw-Hill, $15), and *How and Where to Find the Facts,* by William Sunners (Arco, $7.50). Both should be available in most large libraries and can send

you in many helpful directions in your quest for information.

Magazine articles can also be of great assistance in your research, and you can find thousands of these, classified by subject, author, and title, in the *Readers' Guide to Periodical Literature,* which dates from 1900. Earlier listings may be found in its predecessor, *Poole's Index to Periodical Literature,* covering numerous articles published throughout most of the nineteenth century.

A rich mine of information is operated by our federal government through the Government Printing Office, which publishes books and booklets on almost every conceivable subject. The Superintendent of Documents, Government Printing Office, Washington 25, D. C., will sell you a book itemizing thousands of government publications in print, or you may ask the G.P.O. to place your name on a mailing list to receive (free) a biweekly listing of new books and pamphlets. And, happily, all the material (except in an occasional rare instance, and so documented) issued by the G.P.O. is in the public domain, which means you are free to use it how and where you will without infringing copyright. A writer who uses an actual quotation or draws primarily on research done by someone else of course indicates his sources whether or not the material is in public domain. It is assumed that everything in a manuscript, unless the writer acknowledges the contrary, is compiled and written by the author.

Also, every executive department of the federal government and most state agencies publish material about the activities under their official wings. The U. S. Department of Agriculture, for instance, publishes *Yearbooks* dealing with all aspects of forests, insects, soil, livestock, and other subjects with which the department is directly concerned. The

Yearbooks are among the volumes for sale by the Superintendent of Documents, who will supply a list of them upon request. Many government publications are free. Others may cost anywhere from a nickel to several dollars.

One valuable reference source not to be overlooked is the New York *Times Index,* which is, as it implies, an index of news and feature stories that have appeared in the *Times* over the years.

Incidentally, be sure to read the *Times* or some other good newspaper daily for the express purpose of finding (and clipping) any news items or features relevant to your project. These may provide new leads for further research and will also help to keep you informed of new developments that may be important enough to include in your book.

Interestingly enough, some of the best reference sources are nonfiction books written for children and young people. Such books are written in clear and simple language, are factually accurate, and can be read rather quickly with more enjoyment than profound scholarly works. The latter, of course, are invaluable for intensive analysis of a particular facet.

In gathering information from reference works, *always be sure to get much more than you think you will need.* (For published books of 50,000 or 55,000 words, I usually accumulate at least 100,000 words of typewritten notes, in addition to quantities of printed matter, including some books.) Many facts you unearth will never be incorporated in your manuscript, but they will show up indirectly because they make you more familiar with your subject and enable you to write with a degree and feeling of authority that will transmit itself

to your reader. If some aspect of your subject isn't entirely clear to you, keep digging into more sources until you are sure you understand it.

POINT: *Learn about the research riches available to you in scores of reference books to be found in your local or state public library.*

Be sure to read a good newspaper (or several), with an eye cocked for news items relating to your book idea.

Obviously not all of your notes will be taken from reference works or printed material. On the contrary, you should make every possible effort to collect as many facts as you can at first hand by personal interviews with authorities in the field.

Remember!

- Send out calls for help by mail. Write to industrial firms, professional societies, associations, congressmen, government agencies, and other pertinent organizations, asking for any material that might be relevant to your research.
- Don't overlook museums and historical societies as sources of factual information. The Smithsonian Institution, for example, can tell you almost anything about science and history.
- Make friends with your public librarian. She is a fountain of information, eager to spill over to help you. Remember that if she doesn't have the books you want, she may be able to get them from other libraries or the public library in your state capital.
- Learn about the sources of reference books, available in libraries, from which you can get helpful facts and leads.

9

Planning the Personal Interview

At a highway bus stop a man on crutches, his right leg amputated at the knee, climbed aboard a bus and sat next to a writer. After the bus had rolled along for a few minutes the writer, always curious, turned to his seat mate and nodded toward the half leg.

"The war?" he asked.

The man smiled and shook his head. "Nope," he said.

Two minutes later the writer said, "Automobile accident?"

"Nope."

Half a mile farther the writer spoke again. "I don't mean to pry, but you see——"

The other man interrupted. "Bub, if I tell you how I lost my leg, will you promise not to ask any more questions?"

"I sure will!"

"All right, then. It was bit off."

The writer's eyes betrayed his excitement and eagerness. "Bitten off? How did——"

The man held up one open hand. "Now, now," he said, "you agreed not to ask more questions. Let's drop it, huh?"

POINT: *As a writer, never agree to stop asking questions. Questions, and especially answers, are of prime importance in research for nonfiction books. Obviously the questions should be addressed to people who are qualified to provide the information the writer needs, so one of the first problems is how and where to find such people.*

AUTHORITIES, WHERE ARE YOU?

This is where your preliminary reading and study begin to pay off. When you know something about your subject, you must also have acquired some idea as to the identities and probable whereabouts of a few experts in the field, and you should have absorbed at least a smattering of knowledge that would help you to interrogate them with a reasonable degree of intelligence.

Perhaps, however, you *don't* know the names of individuals, companies, associations, or government agencies in the field you want to write about. How do you find them? In a big city, such as New York, Chicago, Washington, or San Francisco, the Yellow Pages of the telephone directory usually include a listing of "Associations," and you may search its entries for the names of associations of interest to you. Here is a sample listing from the Washington, D. C., Yellow Pages directory (the street addresses are not important for our purposes): "American Association of Retired Persons, Ameri-

can Institute of Architects, National Wildlife Federation, Senior Citizens of America, World Confederation of Organizations of the Teaching Profession."

If you don't live in a big city, and don't have access to a metropolitan telephone directory, go to the business office of the telephone company in your town and ask to see a New York telephone book or one for any large city that is nearby.

If telephone directories are not available, call or visit a store, factory, or business office in your town that deals in goods or services related to your book idea. Such places will probably know about national associations or groups that could be helpful, and perhaps be able to give you names and addresses of officers of such groups.

Your town's chamber of commerce, or your local newspaper office, might have lists of organizations to which you could write for information.

Municipal officers in the county seat of the county in which you live should be able to refer you to appropriate officials and departments of the state government in your state capital. If you want information from some state agency, you might even address an inquiry to the governor, knowing that his office will refer it to the proper source for reply.

Information about every department and agency of the federal government is given in a paperbound book entitled *United States Government Organization Manual.* This volume, published yearly by the Government Printing Office, describes the duties of each federal agency and lists its officers by name and title. The book may be purchased from the Superintendent of Documents (Government Printing Office, Washington 25, D. C.) and should also be available in most public libraries.

When you decide which sources may be helpful in the area you want to write about, approach them personally, or by telephone or letter, asking if they would arrange interviews for you with qualified specialists of their selection. Most big companies and government agencies have public relations departments and are glad to cooperate with writers, often in the hope that favorable publicity will accrue to the organization. Whatever the reasons, I have always had cordial receptions from the scores of public and private establishments in which I sought information and assistance.

POINT: *There are many avenues down which you can find the names of organizations and agencies where you might arrange to interview specialists who can give you needed facts for your book. The federal government's* Organization Manual, *telephone directories, factories, business offices, chambers of commerce, municipal and state officials, among others, make good starting points.*

DIALING AND MAILING

To avoid extensive travel, some writers use the telephone to ask questions of authorities in distant places. If you plan to do so, you should prepare your questions and have them before you when you make your calls.

If it is at all possible, however, I suggest the face-to-face interview rather than phone-to-phone. How does one arrange for such interviews? By telephone or letter. I prefer the letter, because if I cannot find the name of a specific individual in some company, I can address the letter to the company and know that it will be routed to the right person. If I tele-

phoned, I might have to talk to three or four people before I finally reached the one who could help me.

What goes into a letter asking for interviews? To whom should it be addressed? It may be addressed to an individual (preferably one concerned with public relations) or simply to a company or an organization.

For instance, I was asked if I would like to write a book about career opportunities in banking. I knew little or nothing about the banking business. I knew how to make deposits and withdrawals—especially withdrawals!—how to write checks, and how to borrow money. I *didn't* know what went on behind the counters after closing hours, and I didn't know about the many banking activities with which the average depositor isn't concerned.

I read an encyclopedia article about the origin and development of banks and about banking affairs, and a rather dull technical book about banking services, and I talked with a friend who worked in the Federal Reserve System.

Based upon the information I gleaned from these sources, I decided—à la *Goldilocks and the Three Bears*—that I should explore the goings-on in a big bank, a middle-sized bank, and a little bank, because these should provide an insight into almost every kind of bank function and employment area.

Accordingly, I chose to write first to the Chase Manhattan Bank of New York, the second biggest banking institution in the world. I didn't know anyone there, so I asked an officer of a Washington bank, where I had an account, if he could get the name of the individual who supervised public relations work for Chase Manhattan. He found a listing in a bankers' directory and gave me the name of a vice president, to whom I wrote as follows:

Dear Mr.——:

I am the author of a number of books, including several dealing with career opportunities for young men and women in various fields, published by Julian Messner, Inc., of New York City.

I am now exploring the possibility of writing a book about careers in banking. In doing research for such a book I would hope to proceed as I did with other books; that is, I would like to obtain first-hand information about the jobs I describe from the people who are now doing these jobs. For a career book about medical research, I interviewed scientists who were conducting such research. For one about aviation careers I talked with aviation specialists in various phases of the industry.

Before I sign a contract with my publisher to write a book on careers in banking, I am anxious to determine whether there is material which would make such a book interesting as well as informative, and whether I would be able to get the material by personal interviews with bank personnel who would tell me about their work.

The purpose of this letter, therefore, is to ask whether the Chase Manhattan Bank would be willing to cooperate with me in this project by permitting me to talk with representatives of its various departments and activities, with the understanding that whatever I wrote on the basis of these interviews would be submitted to you or to any other officer of the bank for review, in the interests of factual accuracy. If the bank gives favorable consideration to this request, I would appreciate an opportunity first to talk with you or someone you suggest regarding the banking field in general, so that I might decide whether to proceed with my proposed book.

A self-addressed stamped envelope is enclosed for your convenience in replying.

The Chase Manhattan vice president informed me that the bank would be happy to cooperate with me, and a date was set for my arrival. I went to New York City and was introduced to several bank officers, some of whom described various functions in which I might be interested. I was given a desk and a telephone, and permission to talk with whomever I wished, and a memorandum describing my project was sent by the bank to its various departments. After a study of the bank's organization chart, I made appointments with numerous employees and spent several days interviewing them about their work in Chase Manhattan.

My next visit was to the Bank of Damascus, Maryland, which employed eight people, and here I observed the problems and workings of a country bank, which provided a vast contrast to those of the metropolitan giant. One chapter in my book is headed "A Day in Damascus."

For a sort of in-between look, I arranged appointments with officers of the Riggs National Bank in Washington, D. C.—an old institution and a large one, yet smaller, of course, than Chase Manhattan.

In addition, I talked with representatives of the Federal Reserve System, the Comptroller of the Currency, savings banks, savings and loan associations, investment banking associations, and other financial agencies, all of whom were glad to make appointments with me.

POINT: *Use the telephone and the mails to ask questions or to arrange appointments for personal interviews. A letter may be preferable to a telephone call if you don't know the name of some specific individual, because a letter addressed to a business house will be routed to the appropriate em-*

ployee. A telephone call, however, might require conversations with several people before the right one is located.

WHAT ABOUT LETTERS FROM UNPUBLISHED WRITERS?

In writing letters seeking appointments or information, I'm fortunate to be able to identify myself as the author of several books. What about the writer with no books to his credit as yet? What kind of credentials does he need?

In my opinion, the fact that a person cannot point to his published work will be no obstacle in his quest for research information. The author of a dozen books was *once* a no-book writer. Everyone has to begin somewhere.

If you propose to write your first book, there's no reason why the inquiries you make should call attention to the fact that you don't have a string of books in print. Simply identify yourself as a writer and explain what you want to know, perhaps in a way such as this:

Dear Mr.——:

As a free-lance writer I am doing research for a proposed nonfiction book about gambling, with special emphasis on the advantages and disadvantages of legal lotteries.

Although a few books in this field are available for reference, I prefer to obtain as much information as I can by personal talks with people qualified to express intelligent views both for and against nationwide legalized gambling.

Newspaper and magazine articles indicate that you and your associates have recently advocated the institution of a national lottery to help reduce the national debt. I would appreciate an opportunity to talk with you and with others in your organization to obtain material for my proposed book, with the

understanding that I will show you that part of my manuscript that is based upon these interviews, so that I may be sure my statements are factually correct.

If this is agreeable, would you be kind enough to suggest a date and time when it would be convenient for me to call at your office?

A self-addressed stamped envelope is enclosed for your convenience in replying.

It is quite possible that when you conduct your interviews you will be asked what books you have written or what magazines have published your material. If you have never had anything in print, don't be ashamed to say so. If you don't even have a contract as yet for your book on gambling, merely explain that all book publishers require an outline and sample chapters before offering contracts, and that you are in the process of gathering facts to enable you to meet this requirement.

Here, however, you can understand the value and wisdom of getting at least an expression of interest in your book idea from a publisher before you undertake extensive research work. Such an expression will permit you to say, in letters or interviews, that the John Jones Publishing Company, for example, is interested in publishing your proposed book.

Your assurance that you will show the appropriate part of your manuscript to the person interviewed tends to banish any reluctance on his part to speak freely to you. On one occasion an appointment was made for me by a public relations man to talk with a certain authority, but the public relations man was a little nervous about the coming interview.

"He says you can come to his office," he told me, "but that doesn't mean he'll answer your questions. I may as well be frank. This guy doesn't like writers, particularly newspaper reporters, because he's been misquoted on several occasions. Two months ago we arranged for a magazine writer to interview him, and he threw the writer out of his office bodily! I'm telling you this so you'll have some idea of what to expect."

I called at the expert's office before the appointed hour and was ushered in. He was seated at his desk and scowled at me through dark-rimmed spectacles. I spoke his name and was prepared to shake hands, but he leaned back and growled, "What is it you want?"

"I'd like to ask you about your work," I said. "I'm writing a book about career opportunities for young people, and I want to tell them what's involved in a profession such as yours."

"Are you writing this book as an advertisement for some private company?"

"No, sir. It will be one of several I've written on my own for a New York City publisher."

He swung around in his chair and looked out of the window, his back toward me. "I don't like writers," he said. "They distort facts."

"I understand that you've been misquoted on occasion," I said, "but that can't possibly happen in this case because I won't send my manuscript to the publisher until all of the information in it has been double-checked by the people I talk to."

He turned and squinted at me. "You mean you'll show me what you write?"

"I certainly will. It's important to me. When my book comes out, I don't want experts telling my publishers that some of the facts are wrong."

He toyed with a pencil and kept his eyes on it for a minute or more, then looked up at me, nodded, and said, "Have a seat."

We talked for an hour, then he had to go to a meeting. "If you want any more, come back again," he said. I thanked him and we shook hands. "Don't forget," he added, "I'm to see what you write."

Later I showed him the part of the manuscript based upon his statements. He changed two words in it and complimented me on the accuracy of my reporting. When the book was published, I presented him with an autographed copy that he received with a wide grin and the delight of a small boy receiving a birthday present.

POINT: *If you have no publishing credits, don't let that discourage you in seeking information by personal interviews. In letters asking for appointments, you needn't volunteer the fact that you haven't written other books. Simply identify yourself as a writer engaged in research. Later,* if you're asked, *explain briefly that you must do certain preliminary work before a publisher will consider offering a book contract, and that you are hopeful of getting such a contract.*

Remember!

- In doing research, never agree to stop asking questions.
- To find names and addresses of organizations in which you might want to interview specialists about your book idea, use telephone directories, inquire of business of-

fices, factories, chambers of commerce, and municipal, state, or federal officials, among others.

- Consider making telephone calls to acquire information and perhaps save travel expense. If you don't have the name of an individual to call, address a letter to the organization, and it will be routed to the appropriate employee.

- If you are unpublished, you needn't volunteer that information in your correspondence. Merely identify yourself as a writer doing research. If you're asked about your published work, explain briefly that you have none as yet, and that you must get information for an outline and sample chapters to submit for a possible book contract.

- Try to get some evidence of a publisher's interest in your book idea before you undertake extensive research.

10

Conducting the Interview

DON'T BE LATE

Appointments, so far as a writer is concerned, should be held sacred with respect to time. If you agree to call upon someone at two o'clock, don't show up at two-fifteen, or even at two-two. I try always to be on hand at least fifteen minutes early, for I know that time is important to the person I am to see, and that he or she is putting aside regular work to accommodate me.

If for any reason you are unable to keep your appointment at the agreed time and place, telephone the person you were to see, apologize for your inability to meet him, and try to arrange a visit at another hour and date. On the second occasion, only a serious emergency should prevent you from keeping the appointment.

If you can possibly arrange to take your "interviewee" to lunch or dinner, it is quite likely that your visit will be more productive than if it were held in an office. The casual at-

mosphere in a quiet restaurant is more conducive to relaxed conversation than that of the jangling telephones and pickety-pickety of office typewriters.

POINT: *Be early for your appointments. At least don't be late! And if you can't appear as agreed, telephone to apologize and arrange a later visit. Try to conduct your interviews at lunch or dinner, for an easier flow of conversation.*

DO YOUR HOMEWORK FIRST

In preparation for an interview, you will be wise to prepare a few pertinent questions, trying to phrase each so that it cannot be answered fully by a lone "Yes" or "No," but will require a more detailed answer.

For instance, suppose you're to visit the proponent of a national lottery. Here are examples of questions you might ask:

"Why are you convinced that a national lottery would be beneficial to the country? . . . Your opponents claim that a legal lottery would be harmful to low-income families, who would buy tickets with money that should go for food and other necessities. What's your reaction to that argument? . . . How could a lottery be conducted so that the public would be sure the lottery was safe from fraudulent operation? . . . What tangible benefits would accrue to the public and to the government if a national lottery were authorized and put into operation?"

If your book idea concerns complex matters, you should read enough about the particular phase you're going to discuss so that you can frame questions to be asked when you arrive for your interview.

POINT: *In advance of any personal interview, be prepared with intelligent questions on the subject which your source is qualified to discuss.*

KEEP THE TALK ON THE TRACK

Sometimes an interviewer's quarries enjoy talking about matters other than their work, such as families, sports, gardening, backaches, hangovers, ulcers. At the opening of an interview, this kind of conversation can be helpful because it tends to put both you and your source at ease. A certain amount of this small talk may even be useful in your writing, but your primary job is to ask questions relating directly to your book idea, and you should do so as soon as you can.

After you begin your interrogation, your source may again digress. If he does, you must be tactful and ingenious enough to get the interview back on *your* track. If the discussion goes off on enough tangents, you may discover that your allotted time has expired before you have nailed down the information you came to get. Usually you can go along with alien matters for a minute or two, but if the talk strays too far off center, you might deliberately look at your watch (or the office clock, if there is one), turn a page in your notebook, and ask your next direct question, thus steering the subject back to the straightaway.

If you don't clearly understand an answer to a question, come right out and say so. If you're in a fog about some portion of the book you want to write, you can't expect an editor to know what it's all about—and a reader may never get the chance.

POINT: *Keep each interview centered on your book idea. If*

your quarry tends to stray from your subject, use any natu-
ral pause to ask a direct question that will bring him back
to it.

NOTES AND QUOTES

In your interviews, the taking of notes is of great importance. Whether you write with pencil or pen, keep a spare on
hand in case your lead breaks or your ink doesn't last.

The person you're interviewing may make some statements
that aren't significant enough to record. Your task is to be
aware of remarks that merit inclusion in your book. Since
you probably write in longhand, you can't expect to report
every word, but you *must* try to write key words (or abbreviations) that will prod your recollection when you later tran-
scribe and elaborate upon your notes.

For instance, in talking with the advocates of a national
lottery, you might come away with notes such as these:

Contin. Cong. rsd cash by lott. *for* Continental Congress raised
cash by lottery.

Frn ctries succ. Ir. Sw. *for* Foreign countries successful. Irish
Sweepstakes.

Tkts—no force. *for* No one is forced to buy lottery tickets.

Simp. tx chk on wnrs. *for* Lottery would simplify tax checkup
by federal government on winners.

Ppl als gamb. Let gv prft. Pbl bil $ yr. *for* People are always
going to gamble, lawfully or unlawfully. Why not let the
government recognize this fact and rake in a probable billion
dollars yearly from national lottery?

When you hear a statement that would make a good quotation for the book, ask your source if he would permit you to quote him. If he agrees, ask him to repeat his remark slowly enough so that you can write it exactly (to avoid misquoting).

During my interviews I write shorthand notes in a stenographer's notebook, which means that I can record answers practically verbatim. These are later transcribed on the typewriter for easier reference. If you plan to write regularly and to conduct numerous interviews, you might consider taking a course in shorthand or Speedwriting to simplify your note-taking.

Some writers believe that the making of notes of *any* kind is so disturbing to some people that it is wiser for the interviewer to depend upon his memory alone, waiting until he concludes his visit before he writes what he can recall. Like many other aspects of writing, this method may be satisfactory for some and equally unsatisfactory for others, but it seems to me that the interviewer who fails to make notes of any kind is likely to forget important points, and also, quite innocently, to twist certain statements so that when quoted they do not correctly reflect what was actually said.

In the few hundred interviews I've conducted, I have not yet met anyone who objected to my note-taking or who seemed upset by it.

As your writing career progresses, you may want to consider using a portable tape recorder for interviews. This method, used by many successful authors, insures that every question and answer is captured electronically for later replaying or transcribing. This is perhaps the best way to collect oral information, and if I were not a creature of habit with my shorthand method, which serves me most satisfac-

torily, I think I'd choose the electronic interview. I would guess, however, that a microphone might, with some people, generate more reluctance to talk than would note-taking.

POINT: *Take notes when you conduct interviews. Write enough key words or abbreviations to refresh your memory about important facts supplied by your source. As your writing career progresses, consider learning to write shorthand or using a portable tape recorder. Either or both will be useful, not only in interviewing, but also in recording research information for books and other printed material.*

DIG FOR THE ANECDOTE

I'm convinced that one of a writer's most-needed ingredients to make a nonfiction book readable as well as helpful and informative is the personal anecdote, and that in every interview you should strive to dredge up pertinent stories from the lives and work of the persons you question.

In writing, as in life, people are always interested in other people, and a brief anecdote here and there gives a book a sparkle and freshness that lighten and brighten more prosaic expository material. Whenever you hear a formal speech, doesn't your interest sharpen when the speaker says: "I remember one day when I was walking along the street minding my own business, and a man with long red whiskers grabbed me by the arm and . . ." ? The storyteller has been in public favor since the days of King Arthur and before, and continues to be universally popular.

Furthermore, the anecdote often provides an opportunity for the use of dialogue, which not only adds snap, crackle, and pop, but also endows a page with visual appeal; that is,

it helps to break up what might otherwise be long, solid paragraphs of the kind that many readers like to "skip over." In other words, the reader who flips through the pages and sees short bits of dialogue and short paragraphs gets the idea that the book is "easy" to read, and thus perhaps preferable to others on the same subject.

How do you get people to tell you these anecdotal sparklers? Pry a little. Ask questions such as "What's the most difficult problem you've had to solve?" Or, "I'll bet that some funny things have happened to you on this job—what sticks in your mind as the most humorous?" Or, "I'm sure your work isn't all dull and routine. Can you tell me about one or two of your more exciting or unusual jobs or moments?" (This is always productive, because most people don't like to say that their work is "dull and routine," even if it frequently is.)

The interview, as it progresses, should suggest other questions that lead to more anecdotes. For example, the person you're interviewing may make a casual remark, such as: "I enjoy my work today as much as I did when I started in as a youngster, twenty years ago."

That's your cue to ask: "How did you feel the first day you came to work? Were you excited, maybe scared a little?" Or, "Do you remember what you did the first day you came to work?"

The anecdotes, of course, should be pertinent. That is, they should be used only when they have some bearing upon the subject of the book. In my research for *Treasures by the Millions* I talked with Dr. F. H. H. Roberts, Jr., an archaeologist who is Director of the Smithsonian's Bureau of American Ethnology. When I asked him if he had any unusual

experiences in the field, he said he was unable to recall any that might be interesting to the average reader.

"You mean it's all just dull routine?" I asked. "Isn't there ever any excitement? Aren't there sometimes obstacles or hazards?"

After a few thoughtful moments he told me about a camping experience in Arizona which I quoted in the book this way:

"We wouldn't dare go outside at night without a flashlight for fear of stepping on a snake," Dr. Roberts said. "The trouble was, they weren't content to stay outside. One night when I was in bed I saw a big rattler slithering along a beam just above me. Before I could do anything he fell on me. I scrambled out, grabbed a shovel, scooped him outside and killed him."

On some mornings when he slept outdoors in a bedroll Roberts found tracks in the sand where sidewinders had wriggled around him through the night.

This and other experiences of Smithsonian curators served to illustrate some of the less routine aspects of the work they performed in the name of scientific progress and helped to add drama to the book.

In researching *Money Masters* I talked with bank examiners about their work. One told me a story that helped to show what they did and which I used as the opening of a chapter about bank examinations. Here it is:

Jennie Jackson isn't her real name, but she was a real person who became an assistant cashier in a bank where she worked for more than thirty years. She worked hard, often stayed at the bank after others had left for the day, and she was well-liked by her associates and customers.

One day a group of five men appeared at the bank before the doors were opened. When the vice president arrived they introduced themselves as bank examiners and went into the bank with him.

When the bank closed that afternoon they were still there, and Jennie Jackson, with her friendly smile, approached the man in charge.

"I haven't anything special to do this evening," she said. "If you'd like me to stay here and help you I'd be glad to."

"No, thanks, Miss Jackson," the examiner said. "You've done your day's work."

Quickly Jennie answered, "Oh, I don't mind working. I like it. I wouldn't know what to do with time on my hands. Do you know, I haven't even taken a vacation in the past ten years!"

The bank examiners finished their job within a few days and submitted their report, a copy of which went to the bank's board of directors. One recommendation was that hard-working Jennie Jackson be *required* to take some time off, and another was that an audit of the bank be made.

Over her objections Jennie was sent on a three-week leave, and during her absence the audit was made. No suspicions were attached to loyal, lovable Jennie until the completed audit revealed a shortage of more than a hundred thousand dollars in the accounts she supervised.

Throughout her thirty years in the bank there had been many other audits, but during the ten years of her light-fingered operations she had been "Jennie-on-the-spot" to clear up any puzzling facts the auditors turned up, and her glib explanations always satisfied them.

Only the bank examiners' insistence that Jennie be made to take a vacation and that a new audit be made brought about the detection of her embezzlements.

This opening carries the appeal of a detective story, and for the chapter describing the work of bank examiners and auditors I used the heading, "The Bank Detectives."

Here's another anecdote—and I enjoyed this as much as I hope my readers did. I was interviewing Frank Kromholz, a nineteen-year-old who was taking a training course at the Chase Manhattan Bank. Our conversation was in the presence of Frank's supervisor. In the book, after I described the training program and his part in it, I wrote this:

> "Now that you've been here in the bank for eighteen months," I said, "have you decided upon any particular specialty in banking? In years ahead, what would you like to be?"
>
> Rather shyly Frank glanced at the ceiling and answered, "Well—some day I'd like to be president of the bank!"
>
> Chase Manhattan President David Rockefeller, please note.

POINT: *Use personal anecdotes to add sparkle and life to your book. Ask questions about your source's emotions and unusual experiences. Listen for and pursue remarks that could lead to good anecdotal material.*

BE A JOKER ONCE IN A WHILE

Sometimes, depending upon the kind of book to be written, jokes have a place among the anecdotes. Frequently the person being interviewed wants to tell one or two (dealing with his work) that may not be real thigh-slappers, but that he thinks are pretty good or good enough to illustrate a point. A Federal Reserve official with whom I was discussing inflation and deflation told me a joke that I used in *Money Masters* to open a chapter about the Federal Reserve System:

A man told a waiter in a restaurant, "I'll have the five-dollar dinner."

"Okay," the waiter said. "Do you want it on white or rye?"

If we had to pay five dollars for a sandwich, the reason could be stated in a single word: Inflation.

If you think a joke could pep up some portion of your manuscript—and also illustrate a point—try to find an appropriate one in a book of jokes, making whatever switches may be necessary for your special purpose.

POINT: *Most people like to laugh. If you know a joke that can add a light touch to your manuscript and also emphasize a point, use it.*

IS THERE A DARK SIDE?

Whenever you seek information through interviews, it's almost certain that the people who provide it will be strongly inclined to impress you favorably with themselves, their work, and their employers. Sometimes, however, such efforts are masquerades designed to hide truths that may or may not be important to your book, and it becomes your task to uncover as many facets of your subject as you can.

Don't hesitate to ask an employee, for example, to tell you what he *dislikes* about his specialty. Many jobs have disadvantages as well as advantages—fringe boomerangs as well as fringe benefits. Almost any subject has at least two sides, but people sometimes want to discuss only one. A confirmed bachelor can tell you everything that's wrong with marriage, and a husband (especially if his wife's around) can tell you everything that's right with marriage, but it might be difficult to get the bachelor to admit that married life has its good

points or the husband to say that double harness is for the birds.

During research for one of my books—*Nature's Guardians: Your Career in Conservation*—I was reasonably sure that political influence was a strong factor in the appointments of certain officials in county, state, and federal government conservation agencies. In several interviews, I put the question pointblank: "Is your job—or are other jobs in your agency—affected by politics, by changes of administration?"

Many officials in administrative or executive positions pooh-poohed such a thought. Some executives, however, readily admitted that they had been appointed for political reasons, and this is obviously true about most agency or department heads, because their new posts are generally publicized in newspapers when a new administration takes office.

Those in subordinate positions reacted differently. Some insisted that they were "career men" with twenty or thirty years of service to prove it, and this was the truth. Others, though, told me with some degree of caution that changes in political administrations, especially in some states, played havoc with conservation personnel. I learned that even in the federal government, politics could and did affect people who had held responsible posts for long periods.

Since my book was to deal with career opportunities in conservation, I felt duty bound to mention the political hazards. At that time, however, I was myself a federal government employee, and when my manuscript was submitted to conservation agencies to be reviewed for accuracy, it was quite possible that people in high places might object to my comments to such a degree that my own career could be jeopardized. In other words, I could refrain from any blast

about politicians and feel secure, or I could tell the truth and wait.

My book would be read by young people who might seek careers in conservation. If I were not honest, I might as well give up writing. In *Nature's Guardians,* I wrote what I considered to be a fair and impartial view:

> In many government positions—Federal, state, county, and municipal—petty politics may present a real obstacle to the young man who hopes to make a successful career for himself in the conservation field.
>
> In most departments of the Federal government there are some jobs in the higher grades that fall prey to political patronage, no matter what party may be in power. This had not been the case with career employees in the Fish and Wildlife Service until the national administration changed in 1952, when the Secretary of the Interior demoted Mr. Albert M. Day from Director to Assistant Director of the Service, despite the fact that Mr. Day was a recognized international authority on wildlife management and had risen to the top job after some 30 years' service which began as a professional hunter in the field. Mr. Day retired to accept an important post as an officer of the Arctic Institute. The new Director, although a capable administrator, was not a career man in wildlife management.
>
> This is no indictment of any political party. Patronage has always been an important method of paying political debts for the winners in an election, and in the Federal government the possibility exists that every four years some executives will resign either voluntarily, knowing their appointments were originally strictly political, or by request to make room for some of the "deserving faithful." The stated objective is understandable. A new administration wants its policies to be administered by those who believe in them.

In certain states, politics may make changes in jobs at various levels, from Deputy Game Wardens to Directors. As one conservation expert said, "You might be the best game warden a state ever had, but if some influential politician has an unemployed nephew, you might be the best *ex*-game warden in the state!" On the other hand, some state game departments are notably free from political interference on any grand scale.

The spoils system does not disrupt or even affect many agencies, and it is not to be inferred that every high-salaried governmental job, Federal or state, is in jeopardy for political reasons. This is definitely not the case, as many career men have been retained in various posts through administrations of both major political parties. In some instances, executives of opposite political beliefs have been appointed to important Federal government positions.

The fact is, however, that the young man considering a career in governmental conservation work, Federal or state, will do well to raise questions about the security of his future with relation to political practices before he takes his job.

This and other portions of my manuscript were read by officials of the Fish and Wildlife Service, who made a few minor technical corrections in the other portions—but not a single word was changed in the part relating to politics. I was later told by one employee, in confidence, that "some of the top brass definitely didn't like that part," but no one felt free to recommend changes because it was true.

POINT: *Find out everything you can about* all *sides of your subject, and write about the bad as well as the good.*

LOOK AS YOU LISTEN

When conducting interviews, be alert to your surroundings and to the physical appearance and mannerisms of the person you're questioning. Make notes about both. If appropriate, a few words about your quoted expert's pink eyes, green hair, and webbed fingers will make him more of a personality and not just a name. In addition, his string necktie, the trinkets on his desk, the pictures on his walls, his furniture, may offer clues to his character, his likes and dislikes. Of course you may have no need for such descriptive matter, but it can serve to breathe life into your source and give color to your writing.

In researching my Smithsonian book I interviewed Dr. Doris M. Cochran, Curator of the Division of Reptiles and Amphibians. Here is part of that interview as it appears in the book (note the conveying of information through dialogue):

> In her office-laboratory Dr. Cochran sits in the midst of jars of alcohol containing snakes, lizards, turtles, crocodiles, frogs, salamanders, and their relatives. In all, she has about 150,000 specimens.
>
> I saw pickled frogs half as big as footballs and just as brown. Originally bearing brilliant colors, specimens lose coloration in the alcohol and are all about the same chocolate shade.
>
> "Did you catch those frogs yourself?" I asked.
>
> "Yes, I did," Dr. Cochran said.
>
> "I've never seen such whoppers. Where are they from?"
>
> "Colombia."
>
> "How'd you do it?"

"Well, mostly I collected at night, with a flashlight, because frogs are more active at night, especially during the breeding season. The light attracts them. I'd hold it in my left hand and wave it in front of a frog's eyes, then grab him with my right hand."

At the other extreme she showed me some specimens of Villavicencio frogs, also from Colombia, only about one inch long. "They jump sideways," she said, "and they're harder to catch than fleas!"

POINT: *Be alert to your surroundings during interviews. Furnishings, decorations, pictures, desk gadgets—anything may provide clues to the personality of the man or woman you're questioning. Note any unusual physical characteristics or mannerisms, oddities of dress, peculiarities of speech. Maybe these notes won't be useful when you come to write your book—but if they are needed, you'll have them.*

ASK FOR PRINTED MATERIAL

When you conclude an interview with your specialist, ask whether he has any printed material bearing upon his work. A scientist will probably have reprints of articles he has written for technical journals. He may have a scrapbook containing news or feature stories about himself and his accomplishments, or he may be able to provide names and dates of publications in which such articles have appeared (and which you may find in the public library or the company's own library). Sometimes house organs published by various companies carry so-called human interest articles

about employees; ask for several back issues, in which you may find helpful facts, statistics, and stories.

Interviews and other research could go on and on, but the time comes when you must decide that you have enough information to begin sorting out and organizing your collected facts in preparation for the writing of your manuscript. You may find subsequently that more research is required on some phase of the book, but you will be wise to write a rough draft based upon the abundant information you have, and later obtain and fill in any needed facts before writing the final version.

POINT: *It almost never occurs to the person you interview to tell you that printed matter is available concerning himself or his work, so be sure to ask whether he has any. The more material you collect, the better.*

Remember!

- Don't be late for appointments.
- If possible, conduct interviews at lunch or dinner, to induce an easier flow of conversation.
- Prepare a few pertinent questions in advance of an interview.
- Don't be sidetracked by irrelevant conversation.
- Make notes about significant facts—or use a portable tape recorder.
- Strive to obtain personal anecdotes that will lighten your book.
- Use an occasional joke if one is appropriate.

- Note the surroundings, physical appearance, and mannerisms of the people from whom you seek information.
- Ask for any printed matter that might be useful to you.
- Be honest with your material. Show all sides of your subject, but do it impartially.

11

Organizing

SORTING YOUR MATERIAL

The style and pace of your writing cannot hide poor organization, and whatever time and care you devote to putting your facts into the most effective package will be worth every frustrating minute.

In organizing your material it is assumed that you will aim at some wordage goal—that is, an approximate number of words for your completed manuscript. In planning the production of books to come, publishers usually want writers to stay within word limits specified in contracts so that production budgets and costs may be controlled. This means that the writer must be highly selective with respect to what he uses and what he discards.

When the research for my books has been completed I sometimes find that I have collected miniature mountains of printed matter in addition to my notes. With a crayon I print each chapter heading from my book outline on a 3-by-

5-inch card or slip of paper and lay out the cards on a table. Then I wade through pamphlets and other publications I've collected, sorting them into groups under the headings to which they pertain. Some may be so general that they cover a substantial part of the field, so I make one extra caption, *General,* for this type of material.

When this sorting is finished I have a stack of printed matter and a sheaf of typewritten notes for each outlined chapter, plus the *General* grouping. Up to this point I have usually had time only to skim through many of the publications. Now I must read them carefully, marking sentences or paragraphs that might make useful quotations or might inspire additional interviews and supplementary questions, or suggest sources of information I had not previously considered.

If supplementary questions must be asked of people interviewed earlier, I often telephone them, because at the conclusion of my interviews I always ask for this privilege (and for the number and extension to call). As I said earlier, telephone calls can save considerable time and money.

POINT: *Devise a convenient method for sorting printed material into sections—one section for each chapter of your book.*

WHAT WILL YOU DISCARD?

There can be no rules of "Do" or "Don't" for the organization process. This is one "creative" phase of nonfiction writing, and each writer must decide for himself how to mold his material into what he considers a logical, forceful, and readable mass.

Inevitably there will be problems calling for difficult decisions. You may have a wealth of fascinating material for use in one chapter or another, and space limitations that preclude the use of all of it, in which event you will have to decide what portions should be used and what parts discarded. ("Discarded" doesn't mean "thrown away" because whatever you don't include in your book *might* provide the basis for a salable magazine article or articles.) Here again a degree of creativity is required. The question of what to leave out is often more vexing than that of what to put in.

One aspect of your subject may be rather prosaic yet highly important, while another may be relatively unimportant, but bursting with drama or humor or emotional appeal. You might be able to squeeze one into a few words, giving it a minor place when it deserves more, and allowing you to give the other the full treatment. What shall you choose for the major role? The only answer I can give (without reviewing the choices) is, "Choose the one that, in *your* opinion, will help most to achieve the over-all purpose of your book."

POINT: *Only you can decide what facts must be omitted from your manuscript. Keep those which you believe will make a better book.*

WOULD A PREFACE HELP SOLVE YOUR PROBLEM?

In one of my books, *Diary of Democracy: The Story of Political Parties in America,* I tried to show how political parties began and developed in the United States from the time of the Pilgrim Fathers to the administration of President John F. Kennedy. The presentation was chronological, and when I was ready to write about the period 1860–65 I

wrestled with the problem of how much to write about the Civil War. Obviously this great conflict was of tremendous historical importance and I could not ignore it completely; neither could I dwell upon it at length, because I was writing about the origins and development of political parties and not about the Union and the Confederacy. Yet there were serious political implications that had to be considered. What to do?

In my rough draft I tried to dwell upon certain phases of the war that had political overtones or consequences, such as the Emancipation Proclamation of 1863, which outlawed slavery and strengthened the Republican Party. Later, after very careful consideration, I slashed this part of the draft.

In describing pertinent events up to 1860 I had shown the growing rift between pro- and anti-slavery forces. If I chose to dwell upon the progress of the war I could have selected numerous incidents which would lend considerable drama and excitement to my account, but they would not directly have furthered my purpose of showing how political parties were born and grew and sometimes flashed and faded away. I decided to dispose of the Civil War in these few short paragraphs:

> In December, 1860, South Carolina formally seceded from the Union, and early in 1861 other Southern states followed. In March a permanent Constitution was drawn for the Confederate States of America, and Jefferson Davis of Mississippi and Alexander H. Stephens of Georgia were elected President and Vice President of the Confederacy.
>
> On April 12, 1861, a Confederate farmer-volunteer fired the first cannon shot in a bombardment of Fort Sumter in Charleston Harbor, and from the fort came an answering roar from

a cannon fired by Captain Abner Doubleday, "father of the game of baseball." Thus began a shooting war that was to be one of the bloodiest in history.

A great many northern Democrats supported the President and the Republican party in a common cause—saving the Union. This fusion of "War Democrats" and Republicans, known during the war as the "Union" party, gave the Republicans complete control of Congress.

President Lincoln also won the loyal support of William Lloyd Garrison, the abolitionist, and of Lincoln's former rival, Senator Douglas.

It would be a long time before the Democratic party regained its strength. When the Civil War ended in 1865 there were tremendous problems of reconstruction facing the wounded nation—and all kinds of schemers, connivers, crooks and rogues were on the prowl, in politics and out.

This ended one chapter and led into the Reconstruction Period, woman suffrage, Tammany Hall, and other political developments and organizations in the eventful years from 1867 to 1877.

I felt it necessary to make a brief explanation of my presentation in an Introduction to the book that included this paragraph:

I have not attempted to write the entire history of the United States, because my book is primarily about American political parties; but I have tried to sort out events of major political significance and to show their effects upon parties. The Civil War, for example, is mentioned briefly, but the political party activity that preceded and followed it is told in some detail; and this is the plan of the book wherever other pertinent historical events took place.

POINT: *Sometimes, when you must make a difficult choice of important facts, you may consider it necessary or advisable to explain your reasons in a preface or foreword. Such an explanation might forestall reader criticism that would otherwise be forthcoming.*

BOOKS MAY GENERATE USEFUL IDEAS

Whatever the subject of your book, it is probable that other authors have written about it, too, and it will be to your advantage to study the ways in which they organized their facts—not with any intent of imitating, but to spark ideas that might make your own work superior. Actually, whenever you read any nonfiction book or magazine piece, you should do so critically and analytically, observing the methods used by other published writers to convey their messages to a multitude of readers. This kind of study can teach you more than any textbook or writing instructor.

While I was doing research for *Diary of Democracy,* I read two books—*We Elect a President,* by David Weingast, and *The Many Faces of the Civil War,* by Irving Werstein—because I was interested in the ways in which these two authors presented their material. Both books were helpful in some respects. Reading *We Elect a President* made it possible for me to avoid duplicating some of the information Mr. Weingast had used about political parties, a fact that was later pointed out in favorable reviews of his book and mine.

For his chapter headings in *The Many Faces of the Civil War,* Irving Werstein used quotations or parts of quotations from statements made by characters in the text, each quotation reflecting the chapter content. I considered the possi-

bility of doing the same thing, but I didn't, for two reasons:
I would be imitating Mr. Werstein; and my chapters in
Diary of Democracy covered fairly long periods of time and
involved numerous characters and events, so that no one
quotation would appropriately indicate the chapter coverage.
However, I thought, why not use quotations of my own, and
in a different way?

Immediately following formal chapter headings I used
"diary" entries set in italics, as clues to each chapter content.
Not only did this permit me to show the dates covered, but
also it provided an ideal and novel complement to the book
title, *Diary of Democracy*. Here are the three short "diary"
entries opening Chapter 6 ("Republicans and Rebellion"):

*January 1, 1851: Prospects for a Happy New Year are not
bright. The Compromise of 1850 added more fire to the slavery
question, which is growing more serious every day. As if that
isn't bad enough, Elizabeth Stanton and that pantaloon
Bloomer woman are continuing their agitation to give women
the right to vote. Next they'll want to smoke and drink!*

*July 6, 1854: Senator Steve Douglas is boasting that he alone
pushed through the Kansas-Nebraska bill to permit new states
to decide whether they shall be slave or free. As a result of this
law we now have a new political party made up of a coalition
of Whigs, Democrats and Free Soilers. Its members call themselves "Republicans."*

*April 12, 1861: It is reported that the secessionists are bom-
barding Fort Sumter in Charleston Harbor. If the report is
true, then we are at war with ourselves. This crisis will test the
mettle of President Lincoln; may God guide his hand.*

POINT: *Books dealing with the subject you want to write*

about can sometimes engender ideas that will be helpful to you. Read them with this in mind.

A LAST LOOK AT THE OUTLINE

When you have completed the organization of your material, if there are to be many major changes in the original outline you submitted, it might be wise to send the publisher a revised outline, giving your reasons for making the changes and asking whether or not he has any suggestions for improvement or treatment.

The number of hours you spend, and the care you take in preparing for the actual writing of your book will be investments that can pay big dividends. A good, sound structure—be it house, office building, cathedral, short story, magazine article, or book—must be built upon a firm foundation or it may totter and collapse.

POINT: *Your research and your organization of facts constitute the foundation of your book. When you're satisfied that it's strong and straight, let the writing begin.*

Remember!

- Sort your printed material into sections—one for each chapter of your book.
- In deciding what must be omitted and what retained, use those facts that you believe will best serve the over-all purpose of your book.
- Sometimes a preface can be used to explain the reasons that

prompted you to deal with certain portions of your book in a particular way.

- Techniques used by other writers may help you to evolve new and useful devices for your own book.

12

Style, Speech, and Surgery

When you write a book for publication you are, in effect, a manufacturer ("bookmaker" wouldn't sound right here!). You have produced a volume that will be offered for sale in competition with hundreds or thousands of others. This is one good reason your product should be your very best, and one in which you can justifiably take personal pride.

Some writers, particularly beginners, are concerned about their "style." Style is simply the way one writes. If you try to imitate the style of William Faulkner, Ernest Hemingway, J. D. Salinger, Damon Runyon, or some other well-known, the very best you can hope to become is a good copy—never the original. If you say what you want to say in your own way, your style will make your writing distinctive because it *is* original—it's *you* and nobody else.

If you happen to have a good ear for music, it's probable that your style will be smoother than that of a writer who

141

hasn't, because I firmly believe that good prose writing has a kind of rhythm which helps to make reading more enjoyable. For this reason it is often wise to read your material aloud, or to have it read to you. In this way you can detect rhythmic defects, correct them, and thus improve your writing.

Also helpful is variety in sentence and paragraph length. A succession of long, involved sentences in a long paragraph not only discourages a reader, but also threatens monotony. Use mixtures of short and long sentences, short and long paragraphs, including bits of dialogue.

POINT: *Don't try to imitate published writers. Your natural style is what makes your writing distinctive.*

WRITE SIMPLY TO WRITE FORCEFULLY

Perhaps the most important element of a writer's style is simplicity. Many writers and would-be writers are inclined to be "literary" in their word choices. Perhaps they want to be sure their education is showing, or they hope to stun the literary world with doses of a new brand of deathless prose, or maybe they just haven't yet learned that in general short words are far more effective than multisyllabic words and that *simplicity* gives any writing its greatest force.

In *The Responsibilities of the Novelist* (Doubleday, New York, 1903), Frank Norris had this to say about simplicity:

Suppose, for instance, the New Testament was all unwritten and one of us were called upon to tell the world that Christ was born, to tell of how we had seen Him, that this was the Messiah. How the adjectives would marshal upon the page, how the exclamatory phrases would cry out, how we would

elaborate and elaborate, and how our rhetoric would flare and blazen till—so we should imagine—the ear would ring and the very eye would be dazzled; and even then we would believe that our words were all so few and feeble. It is beyond words, we should vociferate. So it would be. That is very true—words of ours. Can you not see how we should dramatize it? We would make a point of the transcendent stillness of the hour, of the deep blue of the Judean midnight, of the liplapping of Galilee, the murmur of Jordan, the peacefulness of sleeping Jerusalem. Then the stars, the descent of the angel, the shepherds—all the accessories. And our narrative would be as commensurate with the subject as the flippant smartness of a "bright" reporter in the Sistine Chapel. We would be striving to cover up our innate incompetence, our impotence to do justice to the mighty theme by elaborateness of design and arabesque intricacy of rhetoric.

But on the other hand—listen:

"The days were accomplished that she should be delivered, and she brought forth her first-born son and wrapped him in swaddling clothes and laid him in a manger, because there was no room for them in the inn."

Simplicity could go no further.

In this comparison Mr. Norris made clever use of contrast by writing one long paragraph of comment, using such words as "transcendent stillness," "commensurate," "elaborateness," and "arabesque intricacy," all of which *magnify* the brevity and simple language of the Biblical passage. Magnification is the end result of contrast, which the shrewd writer will use when he can in dialogue, description, and incident.

In *Effective Revenue Writing*, a federal government publication designed to help Internal Revenue employees write clear, simple correspondence and directives, author Calvin D.

Linton includes this excerpt from a "professional sociological journal":

> In effect it was hypothesized that certain physical data categories including housing types and densities, land use characteristics, and ecological location constitute a scalable content area. This could be called a continuum of residential desirability. Likewise, it was hypothesized that several social data categories, describing the same census tracts, and referring generally to the social stratification system of the city, would also be scalable. This scale could be called a continuum of socioeconomic status. Thirdly, it was hypothesized that there would be a high positive correlation between the scale types on each continuum.

This quotation, says Mr. Linton, "is trying to say only that rich people live in big houses set far apart, and that poor people live in little houses set close together. . . ."

EXPLAIN TECHNICAL TERMS

Whatever your book has to say should be said simply and clearly so that it will not—cannot—be misinterpreted or misunderstood by the reader. There may, of course, be times when you must use technical or trade terms or jargon in writing about specialized fields. In these instances, explain each such term, parenthetically or otherwise, the first time it appears.

In *Engineers Unlimited: Your Career in Engineering*, this was a necessity, not only in the writing but also in my interviews with civil, mechanical, electrical, hydraulic, and other engineers. When they answered my questions I would frequently have to interrupt and say, "Just a minute, please!

Remember, I'm not an engineer. Can you explain that point again in less technical language?"

Here is one example from the book:

Bethlehem [Steel] also made most of the steel and engineered the superstructure for the Greater New Orleans Bridge, the longest cantilever highway bridge in the world. . . .

A simple cantilever is a board that extends beyond its supports. If you stand two bricks on end, a foot apart, and lay an eighteen-inch plank across them so that one end of the plank projects some six inches into space, you have a cantilever structure. The portion of the board between the bricks is called the anchor arm, counterbalancing the projecting part, or cantilever arm.

During one interview with Dr. T. E. Hienton, an agricultural engineer, we talked about radiation studies and he mentioned "plasmas." I had visions of an accident victim hooked up to a suspended bottle of blood plasma that dripped into his veins, but this didn't fit into our discussion and I said so. Dr. Hienton laughed and explained that he was talking about a different kind of plasma. I included his explanation in the book in this fashion:

"Plasmas are not new," Dr. Hienton explained. "Whenever we look at a lighted neon sign we see a plasma. It is produced by an electrical discharge which knocks electrons from the gas atoms in a tube. The released electrons collide with other atoms and produce more ions [electrically charged atoms], and this process goes on until there are enough liberated electrons to make the gas a good conductor of electricity."

During my research for *Disease Detectives* I met a language barrier I was unable to break down. I talked with an

elderly and highly capable scientist who tried to tell me about his laboratory experiments in some detail. Like some other experts he was conditioned by years of work and study to think and to speak in scientific terms which, to him, were as clear as "Scramble two and hold the spuds!" would be to a short-order cook in a roadside diner. At my urging (and interruptions) he twice described certain experiments dealing with ultraviolet light and vitamins, and found it very difficult to translate the language of science into the language of Neal. Subsequently, to get the information I needed for this portion of the book, I had to interview another specialist in the same field who was able to answer my questions in terms I could clearly understand.

POINT: *If you must use technical terms, explain each the first time it appears.*

DO IT IN DIALOGUE

Where I can do so naturally, I write parts of my interviews in dialogue to get more of the visual appeal and sparkle that I mentioned in an earlier chapter. That is, instead of relaying information in the form of exposition, I quote my own questions as well as the replies. This conversational approach banishes the monotony found in some straight exposition, enlivens the text, and shows the reader that he is getting authentic information direct from the lips of the experts. For instance, in *Engineers Unlimited* I quoted a conversation with S. Richard Costa, a young electronics engineer at the Goddard Space Flight Center of the National Aeronautics and Space Administration. The following excerpt shows the use of dialogue to describe some of his duties:

"Just what do you do?" I asked.

"Well, I've been here since I graduated from college thirteen months ago, so I've had only one major job thus far. I'm working with an O.S.O.—an orbiting solar observatory. We have to understand this spacecraft and how it's operating so that we can get usable information from it. We must know what experiments are built into the satellite and how it conducts them."

"From the name 'orbiting solar observatory' I assume this satellite has experiments to study the sun?"

"That's right," Costa said. "It points at the sun during the daytime portion of its orbit. When it is eclipsed by the earth it is night, and the satellite cannot 'see' the sun. The experiments are designed to measure solar activity and radiation during the satellite day."

"How big is this thing?" I asked.

"It weighs four hundred and fifty pounds, is eight feet in diameter with its jets extended, forty-four inches with the jets folded. . . ."

The writing of dialogue is not so easy as it may seem, and if statements in quotation marks are stilted and stiff the quotation marks should be eliminated and the whole thing should be rewritten, either in better dialogue or paraphrased in the writer's own words.

Stilted speech is sometimes heard during radio and television commercials by prominent sports stars or by homemakers and others who try valiantly to read "plugs" written by advertising agencies for sponsored products. The baseball pitcher or star quarterback is introduced as he stands in the locker room facing the TV camera as though it were a firing squad, and recites his lesson or reads it from a teleprompter: "Hello, folks. Yes, sir, I use Slippery Soap. It works like a

charm, is as mild as May, and it gets you clean as a whistle. After a hard game it makes my shower more refreshing. It smells good, too. I like it."

Probably the truth is that the athlete uses soap that some teammate left in the soap-dish, and if you were to ask him whether it was sweet-smelling Slippery Soap he'd say, "Look, Bud, soap is soap. If it gets the grime off, whadda I care what it smells like?"

A writer must realize that too often an ordinary conversation between two people, reported verbatim, would sound boring and befuddled because when we talk we slur and contract words, leave sentences unfinished, interrupt each other, substitute gestures for speech, and sometimes zigzag from subject to subject. Note this young couple's exchange:

HE: I'll pick you up about seven and we'll go to——
SHE: Make it seven-thirty. I gotta help Mom.
HE: [Nods.] I thought we'd——
SHE: I do the dishes for her. Oh, listen . . . did you ask that guy?
HE: What guy?
SHE: You know . . . about the——
HE: Oh, yeh, yeh. I asked him. He said——
SHE: Was he sore or anything?
HE: [Shakes head.] Don't forget.
SHE: Okay. Seven-thirty. Okay. Where are——
HE: Be ready, will you? Last Sa'rday——
SHE: Where we going?
HE: We missed half the feature. [Shrugs.] A movie, ain't we?
SHE: I thought you said dinner before.
HE: Who said?

The writer must be able to retain the flavor of the spoken word and at the same time write dialogue that makes sense

and furthers his purpose. In gathering information for *The Hallelujah Army,* I had a long talk with Major A. Louise Richardson, the officer in charge of a Salvation Army home for unwed mothers, in Flushing, New York. Major Richardson told me about a typical case involving a fourteen-year-old girl named Kathy, and if I wrote it exactly as I heard it, the result would be a kind of expository report from the Major. Instead, I learned as much as possible about Kathy's character and manner of speech, then I chose to translate the story into a dialogue between Major Richardson and Kathy. Here's the story as published:

> Questioned by Major Richardson, Kathy identified the father of her unborn baby as a 16-year-old boy who lived in her neighborhood.
>
> "How did it happen?" the Major asked.
>
> Kathy shrugged. "We were just left alone too much."
>
> "Couldn't you have your friends come to your house?"
>
> "Oh, sure—but not all the time."
>
> "Just what do you mean by being 'alone too much'?"
>
> "Well," Kathy said, "you and a boy go to the bowling alley, or to the movies or someplace, see? And then you run out of money and you can't go anywhere else, so you go home and sit on the couch and look at television. But, gosh, you don't want to watch it all night, so you start talking and pretty soon you start mushing or something, and the next thing you know you're in trouble."
>
> "What about your parents? Weren't they at home most of the time?"
>
> "Well, some of the time. But they both work all day and at night they often go out to a movie, or to play bridge or something. Anyway, if they were home and I wanted to go out someplace I'd just go."

"They wouldn't ask you where you were going, or try to stop you?"

"Oh, they prob'ly would. But that wouldn't matter, because if I made any kind of a fuss they'd give in quick enough. That's the trouble. If I had been living with my grandmother I wouldn't be in this fix now."

"What do you mean by that?"

"Well, my grandmother is strict, see? Real strict. And when I used to spend week-ends at her house she kept tabs on everything I did. I had to be in bed by eleven o'clock, and I couldn't go out at night by myself, and all that sort of stuff. But we had fun, too, because she used to take me to the beach or the movies, or we'd play cards or something. I guess she really cared about what happened to me. I used to think that it was awful, her being so strict, but now I wish I'd been living with her all the time. Then—then I wouldn't be here."

"Suppose your mother and father had told you to stop seeing this boy? Would you have obeyed them?"

Kathy shook her head. "I guess not, because if I wanted to keep on seeing him I'd just keep arguing with my parents and they'd finally give in. They always do."

In telling me about Kathy, Major Richardson commented, "Here was a child saying, 'Please put limits on my activities. Even though I fight about it, don't let me do things I shouldn't.'"

POINT: *Dialogue properly used can make your manuscript more interesting.*

CUT, CUT, CUT

Whether dialogue or exposition, most writing can be improved by careful cutting. Cutting words, sentences, para-

graphs, or even whole pages from a manuscript may be painful to some writers, particularly if they have labored long and lovingly to produce the material that should be excised. In most instances, however, the surgery will result in noticeable improvement.

What's to be cut? If you have used three or four words to say what one word could, cut the three or four and use the one. For example, at the beginning of this chapter in my *first* draft of this book I wrote: "This is one good reason your product should be the very best you are capable of making. . . ." In the final version I cut the five words, "you are capable of making," and changed the sentence to read: "This is one good reason your product should be your very best. . . ."

Sometimes an incident gets more wordage than it merits. In *From Spinning Wheel to Spacecraft* I wrote about Charles Goodyear's efforts to sell a metal valve for use in rubber life preservers to a New York rubber-goods firm, and my original version of the incident read:

> He found the company officials worried and dejected, and although they looked at his valve they shook their heads slowly and sorrowfully.
>
> "Mr. Goodyear," the manager told him, "a few months ago we might have considered buying your valve. Today our only concern is whether or not we'll still be in business tomorrow."
>
> "But I understood you were doing very well," Goodyear said.
>
> "So we were—for a time. Now we've suffered a disaster. A veritable disaster."
>
> "I'm sorry," Goodyear said. "May I ask what happened?"

The manager stared at him for a moment, then sighed and stood up. "Come with me," he said.

They walked to the back of the building, where many of the rubber goods were stored. Goodyear was almost sickened by a foul odor and put his handkerchief over his nose. "What's that horrible smell?" he asked.

The manager scowled. "Smell, you say? You mean stink, don't you? That's what it is—a terrible stink!" He opened a door to a room filled with shelves, adding, "And this is what makes it."

On the shelves were what had been rubber coats, rubber hats, rubber shoes, rubber life-preservers and other rubber goods. Many looked almost like gooey blobs of tar, and when Goodyear touched some of them he found that they were soft and sticky.

"It melted?" he asked.

The manager nodded. "It melted. Just from the summer heat. Some of our customers brought back rubber suspenders that were melted simply by body heat. Up to now our customers have returned more than twenty thousand dollars' worth of stuff that went bad. In fact it went so bad we had to bury it!"

Goodyear shook his head. "That's truly unfortunate. I'm very sorry, sir."

The manager shrugged. "Well, now you know why we can't buy your valve. Maybe some day you'll have better luck. After all, a lot of people are working with rubber, trying to learn what would prevent something like this. Somebody will find the answer soon—I hope!" . . .

My editor pointed out that this incident was relatively unimportant and suggested that it might be shortened to advantage. I rewrote it this way:

[Goodyear] was shocked to discover that the store was on the verge of going out of business. Its stock of rubber coats, rubber hats, rubber shoes and other rubber goods had melted in the summer heat and oozed into sticky, shapeless blobs. The distraught manager thought Goodyear's valve had possibilities, but obviously the store was not interested in buying it.

Every writer can generally find some portions of another author's book that might be improved by cutting. The point is that *you* should make cuts in your *own* work wherever cutting can improve it. And to do this effectively you must read your material objectively and with word surgery in mind.

DON'T USE LANGUAGE "AS OLD AS THE HILLS"

Word surgery should definitely eliminate all clichés, trite expressions such as *clear as a bell, sharp as a tack, hard as nails, green with envy, bolt from the blue, the worse for wear,* and *crack of dawn.* Editors pay for new and original ways of expressing ideas and facts, and the professional writer strives to be original. Beware of the cliché, the unmistakable mark of the lazy craftsman.

POINT: *Judicious cutting of words, sentences, paragraphs, or even whole pages often improves a manuscript. And strive to use fresh expressions.*

Remember!

• If you try to imitate the style of other writers, your work can be no more than a second-rate copy of theirs. Find your own way to express your thoughts. Be yourself.

- Simple writing is the most forceful writing. Don't use a four-syllable word where a one-syllable term will fit.
- If you must use a technical term, explain it in simple language.
- Consider the use of dialogue where it might add zest to your material.
- Don't be afraid to cut words from your manuscript. Cutting usually makes good writing better.
- Stay away from clichés. If necessary, coin new words to make your work fresh and original.

13

Fiction, Figures, and Failings

THE SHORT STORY PATTERN

Many writers of nonfiction make effective use of fiction techniques in books and magazine articles, because the fiction approach can give dramatic impact and color to descriptions of incidents and events that might lose luster if told in more prosaic fashion.

Most of the short stories in our popular magazines and most of the dramatic tales portrayed on television, in movies, and on the stage follow a pattern—*not a formula,* but a pattern that has been fashioned through years of trial and error, representing an effective way to tell a story that will hold the attention of an audience. This pattern is made up of six segments:

1. MEETING
2. PURPOSE
3. STRUGGLE
4. DARK MOMENT
5. FINAL ACT
6. RESULT

Briefly, here is what they mean:

(1) There is a MEETING of two forces—perhaps man against man, man against beast, beast against beast, man against nature, man against conscience.

(2) One of these forces has a PURPOSE which is *usually* noble. This force thus becomes the hero, the opposing force the villain.

(3) To achieve the purpose, the heroic force must STRUGGLE against odds and obstacles. The struggle provides conflict, which builds suspense. Of course the conflict may be mental rather than physical, but if there is no conflict, you have no story. Any element of struggle helps to retain reader interest.

(4) At a rising point of the conflict the heroic force is threatened by utter defeat. In this DARK MOMENT it appears that his struggle has been in vain and that his opposing force will be victorious.

(5) The heroic force now performs one FINAL ACT to save himself and win his fight. This cannot be a coincidence, nor can it depend upon an unexpected act of God, but must be an action which is in keeping with the dominant trait of the character and which he himself performs.

(6) The RESULT is the achievement of the purpose for which his struggle has been waged. (Sometimes the character may *deliberately* abandon the purpose, or wilfully fail, as a sacrifice to benefit another, in which case he becomes the "tragic hero.")

This technique was ideal for describing certain criminal activities in another of my books, *Six Against Crime: Treasury Agencies in Action.* One case, for instance, told how Gabriel Damone, who had come into the Secret Service from

the detective division of the Pittsburgh Police Department, worked under cover to infiltrate a gang of counterfeiters and negotiated to buy $50,000 in bogus bills from the ringleader, Tony Scalzi.

Using dialogue I described a night meeting between Damone and Scalzi in which the latter insisted upon taking Damone for a ride. The two entered Scalzi's car and drove into the country, shadowed at a respectful distance by Secret Service agents in another car. Soon Scalzi turned off the main highway onto a dirt road in open country, where the agents could not follow without being discovered. The undercover agent was on his own.

They drove to an isolated farmhouse, where Scalzi's accomplices and their women had prepared a dinner to celebrate the "big deal" scheduled to be completed with Damone on the following day. Here is the rest of the story as it appears in the book:

> Feeling considerably relieved, Damone joked and talked with his hosts. Before the dinner was served he saw one of the women whisper something to Scalzi, who went with her into the kitchen. A few minutes later Scalzi emerged and went directly to Damone. Scalzi's eyes were cold and angry. In a low voice he said, "Joe, I want to talk to you. Private." His strong fingers grabbed Damone's arm and guided him into the kitchen. There Damone saw the woman who had whispered to Scalzi.
>
> Scalzi let go of the agent's arm. "Go ahead," he said to the woman. "Tell him what you just told me."
>
> She stepped nearer and faced Damone, a sneer on her lips. "Your name ain't Joe," she said. "You're Gabriel Damone. You're a cop from Pittsburgh. I seen you there in court once."

A hundred thoughts bubbled through Damone's mind and burst. There was no time to think, for if he groped for a defense he would surely betray himself.

Calmly he stared at the woman and at Scalzi, and a grin grew into a chuckle as he began to stroke his black mustache with one finger, first on one side, then on the other.

"I knew I should have shaved off this mustache," he said. "This is the third time I've been mistaken for that cop. I guess I must look something like him, all right, but it's the mustache that does it. He's got a mustache like mine, hasn't he?"

The woman nodded.

"You say you ain't Damone, huh?" Scalzi demanded.

"Tony," the agent said with a tone of disgust, "you ought to know better. I've never even seen the guy. Besides, if I was a cop in Pittsburgh, what would I be doing here in Scranton? Would I have come out to this place with you—alone? You know about my connections in New York—and here, look at my stuff." He pulled out his wallet and began laying cards on the table, a driver's license, membership cards, a Social Security card—all in his assumed name. He glanced at the woman. "I don't blame her, though. I told you I've been taken for this cop before. Look," he added, hiding his mustache with one finger, "now do I look like him?"

The woman took two or three steps to the right, then to the left, her eyes intent upon the agent's face and figure. Finally she looked at Scalzi, shrugged and made a face as though to say, "Maybe I was wrong."

"Is it him or not?" Scalzi asked.

The woman picked up some of the identification cards and examined them closely. "I could have sworn it was him. But it was seven years ago I seen him."

"Yes or no?" Scalzi growled. "This is important, Maria!"

After another glance at the smiling—and anxious—Damone, she said, "No. I guess I didn't remember so well. I'm sorry, Joe."

So the dinner went off as planned, and the next afternoon Scalzi delivered the fifty thousand dollars in counterfeit bills to Damone. The instant the package changed hands Damone placed Scalzi under arrest and signaled other agents, who came to his aid.

An angry Scalzi spat at Damone. "I should have listened to Maria last night," he said. "If I had believed her, you would be where you belong—buried in the pigpen on the farm."

This incident had all the elements of the short story—the forces of law and order in conflict with those of the underworld, a dramatic "dark moment," the final act, and the achievement of purpose.

POINT: *In writing about people and events, search for places in which you might improve your manuscript by using fiction techniques.*

DON'T HOARD YOUR FACTS

Whatever your method of presentation there is one pitfall to be avoided, especially by the writer of nonfiction. It is the failure to write facts which are often so familiar that they are taken for granted, except by the reader. In other words, a writer may be so close to his material that he innocently withholds information that would clarify statements which are otherwise hazy or incomplete.

A resident of Washington, D. C., writing an article aimed at visitors to the capital, said, "The White House is usually near the top of the list of buildings to be visited by sight-

seers, and it is open to the public every day except Sunday and Monday."

This was later changed to show that the White House was ". . . open to the public from 9:30 A.M. to 12:00 noon every day except Sunday and Monday."

If you wrote, "Every morning in his car on the way to his office Mr. Smith makes a final review of the preceding day's reports," some readers might wonder how he does this while driving an automobile at the same time. It would be clearer to say, "Every morning in his *chauffeur-driven* car. . . ."

At one time or another most writers have been guilty of small oversights which can make big differences in clarity. My wife usually reads my rough drafts and has, on occasion, called attention to statements that she finds confusing; I promptly clarify these by revising or adding a sentence or two. This is one advantage to be gained from having your manuscript read objectively by a person who is a layman in the field about which you are writing.

POINT: *Take care not to store facts in your head that ought to be in your manuscript.*

WRITE ABOUT MORE THAN YOU HEAR AND SEE

Another area often neglected in nonfiction writing is that of sensory impressions. Many writers make notes of what they hear and see, but fail to note what they smell, or touch, or taste in the course of their research. Descriptive passages that include impressions of as many of the five senses as possible help to make scenes and backgrounds come alive for the reader.

In *Treasures by the Millions,* I wrote about an interview

with Dr. D. H. Johnson, Curator of the Division of Mammals
in the Smithsonian, who showed me his collections of animal
skulls and skins. In part I said:

> As Dr. Johnson opened various cases to show me their con-
> tents, the air was filled with a pungent and rather unpleasant
> odor, caused by a mixture of ethylene dichloride and carbon
> tetrachloride used as a fumigant to protect the specimens. The
> skins of small specimens, such as mice, are not tanned but are
> treated with arsenic and stuffed with cotton, with wires in tails
> and legs to keep them straight. The arsenic also smells!

Another paragraph included this sentence: "On a live
whale a strip of skin could easily be scraped off the blubber
with a fingernail."

In *The Hallelujah Army,* I described the work of Salvation
Army officers in New York's Bowery Corps, mentioned body
odors emanating from the derelicts, and included this information:

> Body perspiration is almost perfume compared to other
> smells radiating from some men who come to Hoffman for
> help.
>
> "Some of them sleep in doorways or on sidewalks for six
> months or more without a bath or a change of clothing," he
> explained. "They urinate and defecate in their pants. One
> man who came here recently had to walk with his legs wide
> apart because his inner thighs were actually raw from urine
> and fecal matter. We bathed him, coated his burns with oint-
> ment, gave him a change of clothing and a meal, and hope
> that he may come back to let us help him."

POINT: *You have five senses, and they're always at work. Be
especially conscious of them in your research and your writ-*

ing. If you interview someone who tells you of some highly dramatic or thrilling experience ask him about his feelings, his emotions, his thoughts at the height of the adventure or ordeal. They will help to make your written account more vivid, more readable.

SUGAR-COAT YOUR STATISTICS

Readable prose can sometimes be smothered by blankets of statistics, and this is one more ingredient that can be made palatable, even enjoyable, by the alert nonfiction writer. In *Money Masters,* I wanted to begin the book by explaining the functions of a bank in financing a business. This could be set out by the use of banking language and references to formal loans and such, but this kind of beginning would be weaker than boarding-house soup, so I chose to start with a story technique, like this:

> Freddie Smith, the ten-year-old son of a bank officer, wanted to go to a Saturday afternoon movie to see a favorite cowboy star, but the price of admission was 25 cents and Freddie didn't have a dime. He did, however, have an idea which he considered as hot as the August sun that brightened his perspiring face.
>
> In the kitchen at his home he persuaded his mother to set him up in business. She loaned him 30 cents to buy six lemons and 12 cents to buy a pound of sugar for making lemonade, and she agreed to buy back any sugar he did not use. She also contributed eight glasses, a large pitcher, a spoon, and a pail in which the glasses could be washed.
>
> At Henry Jackson's grocery, where Freddie bought the lemons and sugar, he asked for and was given two wooden boxes.

Back home he made his lemonade (using half a pound of sugar), put a lot of ice cubes in it, penciled the words LEMON-ADE 10¢ on a piece of cardboard, loaded everything in his small cart and headed for the bus terminal some eight blocks from his home. Using the wooden boxes as a counter he set up his stand.

Before one o'clock Freddie had sold his tenth and last glass of lemonade, making his receipts total exactly one dollar. He was now a full-fledged "capitalist," for he had decided what kind of business to go into, had made an important business decision as to where to locate his stand, had taken the risk of a possible loss, and had come out with a profit. He repaid his mother 30 cents for the lemons and 6 cents for the half pound of sugar he used, leaving him a gain of 64 cents. He gulped down a sandwich and a glass of milk and rushed off to the movies.

Even Freddie didn't realize how many other people were involved in his business transactions. Henry Jackson, the grocer, would order more lemons and sugar, which meant more trade for owners of a California lemon grove and for some grower of sugar cane in Puerto Rico. Ships, trains, and trucks to carry this merchandise were part of Freddie's lemonade stand —and out in Hollywood the cowboy whose movies Freddie enjoyed so much was making a new picture because Freddie and thousands of other people were paying money to theater owners, who employed many people, who bought many goods. . . .

Of course if Freddie had paid interest on his loan, or rent on his equipment or location, his net profit would have been much less. As it was, his venture turned out well, thanks to his mother, who was perhaps the most important figure in the entire enterprise. She had loaned her son the necessary capital and equipment because she was quite sure his idea was good

and that he would pay her back. In other words, she actually took the place of a bank.

A bank is a kind of store that deals in money. . . .

POINT: *Raw statistics can give readers mental indigestion. If you must use statistics, try to present them painlessly.*

LET YOUR ROUGH DRAFT "COOK"

When your rough draft is completed, the best thing you can do is to put it aside for perhaps a week or more before you look at it again. Then you will probably read it more objectively and thus find words, sentences, paragraphs, or maybe pages that can be deleted, expanded, or otherwise revised for a more effective presentation.

POINT: *Don't rush to polish your first draft as soon as it's finished. In your eagerness, you are likely to overlook areas in which improvements can and ought to be made.*

Remember!

* Fiction techniques can help to add dramatic impact and color to parts of your nonfiction book.
* Beware of hoarding in your head familiar facts that should be in your manuscript.
* Be conscious of the five senses in your research and writing. Whenever possible, describe sensations of taste, touch, and smell, in addition to those of sight and sound, for these will make your writing more vivid to the reader.
* If you must use statistics in your book, dress them up in readable prose as much as you can.

• When you finish writing the first draft of your manuscript, put it aside for several days before you try to see how and where it might be improved. Your viewpoint will be more objective, your eye more critical, and the results more satisfactory.

14

Illustrations

If your book is to include photographic illustrations, obtaining the photographs is your task, not the publisher's. Frequently you can get all necessary pictures without cost, although there may be times when you will have to buy prints to supplement those that are given to you.

If illustrations are to be a part of your book, they should be the best you can get. When you are using photographs, you should obtain many more than will eventually appear in the book, so that the publisher will be able to make a good selection and not be restricted by a dearth of pictures.

For publication, black-and-white photographs should have a glossy finish and be 8 by 10 inches in size, although 5-by-7-inch prints may be usable. Any smaller size is not recommended.

How do you go about getting free photographs?

In doing research for your book, if you get information

167

and assistance from a commercial firm, it is probable that the company can provide a variety of publicity photographs relating to its own activities. For example, I did considerable research at a division of the Westinghouse Electric Corporation near Baltimore, Maryland, for my book about careers in engineering. Appointments with engineers were made for me by William T. Crawford, of the company's public relations department, and when I conducted my interviews I'd ask myself, "Would this engineer's specialty have good pictorial possibilities?" In fact, after *every* interview I asked Bill Crawford if photographs were available to illustrate some of the points we had discussed, and in practically every instance they were.

When my research was ended, Mr. Crawford pulled scores of photographs from the company files, and we looked through them together, picking out those which related to the subjects I had explored during my interviews.

On what basis were my selections made? Whenever possible, I tried to choose a picture not only related to my subject, but also showing people *doing* something. A photograph of the control system of a guided missile is static—but it takes on life if it includes the figure of a shirt-sleeved workman bending over it, with a screwdriver in one hand. In addition, when people are shown in photographs, they provide a basis for contrast, for measurement, for comparison with objects in the same picture. An enlarged photo of a tiny transistor could be made to fill an entire book page, but it would be much more interesting if the transistor were shown between the thumb and forefinger of a human hand.

In instances where there were several prints of the same photograph, Mr. Crawford gave me copies on the spot. If only

one file print was available, he made a note of its identification number and later had a print made and mailed to me.

I went through a similar routine in other engineering firms I visited, all of which were glad to provide photographs of their technical operations. When desired photographs were not available, the company representatives sometimes offered to (and did) have some made especially for my purposes.

I have been given hearty cooperation in obtaining facts and pictures from such industrial giants as the General Electric Company, the American Telephone & Telegraph Company, the Bell Telephone Laboratories, General Motors Corporation, Gulf Oil Company, Raytheon Company, Bethlehem Steel Company, United States Steel, the Radio Corporation of America, and DuPont deNemours, among others.

If your book relates to activities of the federal government, you can get free photographs from many of its departments and agencies. For *Nature's Guardians: Your Career in Conservation* (Julian Messner, Inc., New York, 1956), I obtained excellent pictures from the U.S. Fish and Wildlife Service, Department of the Interior, and from the U.S. Forest Service and the Soil Conservation Service, both in the Department of Agriculture.

For *Pathfinders, U.S.A.,* I used photographs provided free by the Bureau of Public Roads, the Federal Aviation Agency, the U.S. Coast and Geodetic Survey, the U.S. Maritime Commission, and the U.S. Weather Bureau, all agencies of the Department of Commerce. Some shipping pictures were also obtained without cost from United States Lines.

The photographs in *Skyblazers: Your Career in Aviation* (Julian Messner, Inc., New York, 1958) were given to me by the United States Army, Navy, and Air Force, as well as by

commercial aircraft manufacturers and airlines. All of the military services have extensive photographic files in which prints of nonclassified pictures are available to writers.

Photographs of scientists at work, as published in *Disease Detectives,* were supplied by the National Institutes of Health, the U.S. Public Health Service, and by several manufacturers of drugs and medicines, all without charge.

Most federal agencies maintain public relations sections or public information officers who are usually glad to provide writers with facts and photos. If you cannot visit their offices, write letters to the appropriate agencies describing pictures you are seeking, and asking for their help. If they do not have what you need, they may be able to suggest other sources for you to explore.

The point is that you can usually get free photographs on almost any subject, simply for the asking. If you want free pictures relating to chemists and chemistry, write to a big chemical company such as DuPont deNemours or Dow, or perhaps to the U.S. Bureau of Standards, giving a full description of your needs and explaining how the pictures will be used. For photos of aircraft or spacecraft in production or flight, go to aircraft manufacturers, or the Federal Aviation Agency, or the National Aeronautics and Space Administration (N.A.S.A.). For shots of farming implements and farmers, try equipment manufacturers such as John Deere, McCormick, and International Harvester, as well as the state and federal agricultural departments. For pictures of social welfare activities, try the Department of Health, Education and Welfare, or the Salvation Army, or your local Community Chest. Textile manufacturers, mining companies, steamship lines, automobile makers, glass manufacturers, and

other commercial establishments usually have good photographs of their methods and products which they will send out to writers without charge.

In obtaining free photographs, you may be asked to return certain prints when your publisher has finished with them. When you submit your completed manuscript and illustrations, your publisher will make his selection of the prints to be used and return to you those which are found unsuitable. After the book is published, he will return to you the photographs that were used in your book. At this point, be sure that you return to the original source all pictures for which a return request has been made. In the event that it is not possible for you to retain the original glossies as long as necessary to fill your publisher's needs, have copies made for his use. Copies can be made by any dealer who develops and prints film. Obviously, it is best to use the original print, because any copy of a print is likely to lose some clarity and detail.

POINT: *Every writer has scores of opportunities to obtain good photographs, free of charge, from industrial firms in every field and also from state and federal (and sometimes municipal) government departments and agencies. Before you set out to buy photographs for your book, exhaust the possibilities of getting them free.*

CHOOSING THE RIGHT PICTURES

Clarity and detail are extremely important in book illustrations. You must keep this uppermost in your mind when you choose photographs, because an 8-by-10-inch picture may, in its published form, be only a 2-by-3-inch reproduction. In

that event, objects which are small in the original photograph will be almost invisible on the book page.

Also, try to get pictures which have strong contrasts in light and dark, because light shades will be even lighter when printed, and important features may be lost. In some instances, of course, a photograph may portray a scene, person, or activity in which fine detail is relatively unimportant, but do bear in mind that the better the print the better the reproduction.

There may be other points to weigh. Do you want a picture to show an individual or a machine? If it shows both, does it do so in a way that serves your purpose? Should a woman or child be part of the picture? Does it show anything that will date it—such as a calendar on the wall? If so, don't use it. Above all, will it add interest to your book?

POINT: *In selecting photographs, watch for clarity and contrasts, keeping in mind the values that can be lost when the original photograph is reproduced in a reduced size.*

WHERE CAN YOU BUY PHOTOGRAPHS?

If your book requires historical pictures, one excellent source from which they may be purchased at reasonable prices is the Division of Prints and Photographs of the Library of Congress in Washington.

This collection contains millions of photographic prints in every conceivable category, including reproductions of medieval engravings and illustrations from ancient books and manuscripts. In those instances where the library has negatives on file, it sells 8-by-10-inch glossy prints for sixty-five cents each. If a negative must be made, the resulting print

costs $2.65. Pictures from the collection may be published freely, because their copyrights, if any, have expired. A catalogue describing the collection may be purchased for $1.25 from the Division of Prints and Photographs, Library of Congress, Washington 25, D.C.

The New York Public Library (and other public libraries in big cities) also sells prints of photographs that are no longer protected by copyright.

Another important government source of pictures is the National Archives, which contains photographs that cover a vast expanse of American history, especially the activities of the federal government. Glossy prints are sold by the National Archives for $1 each. The Archives Building is at Ninth Street and Constitution Avenue, N.W., Washington 25, D.C., and requests for photographs are handled by the Still Pictures Branch, Audio-Visual Records Division.

The Smithsonian Institution maintains an extensive photographic collection of its countless exhibits and of its scientists at work. It sells prints for seventy-five cents each.

There are a number of commercial firms which sell prints of news photographs or pictures of historic interest. Among these are:

Bettmann Archive, Inc., 136 E. 57th Street, New York, N.Y.

Black Star Publishing Co., 450 Park Avenue, S., New York, N.Y.

Brown Brothers, 220 W. 42nd Street, New York, N.Y.

Freelance Photographers' Guild, 110 W. 32nd Street, New York, N.Y.

Harris & Ewing, 1304 G Street, N.W., Washington, D.C.

Underwood & Underwood, 3 W. 46th Street, New York, N.Y.

Prints obtained from these firms for publication may range in price anywhere from $10 to $15 and up, per print.

One photographic firm, Ewing Galloway (420 Lexington Avenue, New York 17, New York) sells what it calls "stock photographs" covering a wide variety of subjects, and publishes a ninety-six-page catalogue filled with miniature reproductions of the photographs it offers for sale.

Newspapers or wire services (Associated Press, through its picture department Wide World, United Press International, Scripps-Howard, etc.) often sell prints of news pictures taken by their staff photographers. If, while doing your research, you see a newspaper picture you might want, make a note of the date of the paper in which it appeared, the page number, the caption used, and the name of the photographer, if it is given, along with a brief description of the picture. This information will make it easy for editors to identify the pictures if and when you try to purchase their prints. If you do not know exactly what you want, they will make available to you their files on any person or subject, from which you may make your selection.

Most commercial photographic firms have a similar service. Payment is made for only the photographs used, and the others are returned to the dealer. For this reason, it is important that the writer keep a complete and detailed description of *every* picture he obtains "on approval" from a commercial agency. When he returns unwanted prints, there should be no misunderstanding about the number and description of those for which he must pay.

Unless it is otherwise specifically agreed, all illustrative material must be supplied by the writer, which means that

expenditures for photographs, etc., come from the writer's pocket.

POINT: *If you must buy photographs, try first to purchase them from the Library of Congress, the Smithsonian, the National Archives (all in Washington, D.C.), or from other libraries or museums whose prices are low. If satisfactory pictures aren't available at these places, go to one of the commercial photographic firms, or to a newspaper—or take your own!*

BE YOUR OWN PHOTOGRAPHER

You can always try to take your own photographs, and with reasonable amateur skill you can get exactly the shots you need and also save time and money. Modern fixed-focus cameras (many with built-in flash) can produce good pictures and are inexpensive. Other more intricate cameras are more adaptable, of course, and can be a boon to the writer who knows how to use them. Some use the Polaroid Land camera, which takes, develops, and prints a picture within seconds. This has the advantage of permitting the photographer to make sure on the spot that he has the scene he wants, whereas with other cameras he must wait until the film is developed in a laboratory or darkroom to see whether it is satisfactory for his purpose. The Polaroid produces snapshot-size prints, but enlargements may be made with special equipment.

POINT: *You may be able to take the pictures you need with your own camera—even if it's an inexpensive fixed-focus model.*

USING THE CAMERA

I have taken some of the photographs for my books, although my knowledge of photography is not expert. I have a 35-millimeter camera and a $2\frac{1}{4}$-by-$2\frac{1}{4}''$ reflex camera, and I prefer to use the latter for taking pictures to be submitted for book publication. The larger negatives produce clearer enlargements than those of the 35-millimeter size, although many professional photographers use 35-millimeter equipment with great success. Individual preference will govern the kind of camera you use.

If you propose to buy a camera for use in connection with your writing, I recommend that before doing so you talk with a professional photographer, an instructor in a photography class, or the owner or manager of a good camera shop. Explain just what you want a camera for, and ask the expert's advice as to what kind will best serve your purpose.

The lens openings (exposure apertures) of many modern cameras are controlled by built-in light meters. These are light-sensitive cells that automatically set the lens at the proper opening for the light on the subject to be photographed. My camera is not equipped with such a device, so I use a separate light meter to avoid guesswork. The light meter is also a light-sensitive cell, and when set for the proper film speed and aimed at the subject, it activates a needle which points to a number on a dial. By manually rotating a corresponding dial on the meter so that an arrow points to the number indicated by the needle, the photographer is immediately given the choice of a series of "F-stops," or lens openings, each with a corresponding shutter speed for what

should be a perfect exposure. He then merely adjusts his camera settings accordingly.

I cannot, as I say, lay claim to being a skilled photographer in any sense of the word, yet I have managed to take pictures of sufficient quality to be acceptable for reproduction. I learned rather quickly that the use of flash bulbs for interior photographs had drawbacks. For example, I was not at first conscious of the fact that a flash exposure in a room might produce an unusable picture if the flash itself is reflected by the glass in a window, or in a framed picture, or by some shiny object such as a silver table lamp. The reflection "bounces" back into the lens, with the result that the picture one hoped to get is lost in a blot of dazzling light.

To avoid this hazard I learned to use Kodak Tri-X film, which is so fast (sensitive) that it can be used for interior photographs with ordinary light. Even so, I had to be careful about reflections. I took several pictures with Tri-X film in the Smithsonian Institution for use in my book *Treasures by the Millions.* Some of these were of objects displayed in glass cases, and I found it difficult to find an angle at which the pictures could be taken without revealing a reflected image of myself with camera, or reflections of other cases or people. I stood in several different positions and even knelt on the floor, searching the view finder for the ones in which reflections were minimized or eliminated. If you're going to take pictures in places where there are glass or highly polished surfaces, be careful about the reflections.

The Smithsonian displays did not lend themselves to the preferred so-called "action shots," although whenever possible you should try to get some feeling of action into your photographs. A "candid" photograph of a man drinking cof-

fee, or lighting a cigarette, or even talking into a telephone, is much more alive than a formal posed portrait.

The technical requirements for reproduction are somewhat different from those for the family album. First, the pictures must be sharp and have clean detail. This means that you start with a good lens and avoid camera shake and subject Saint Vitus. No photographer, who has to breathe occasionally, can hold a camera still enough at any speed under 1/50th of a second, and even 1/50th is borderline— 1/100th is safer. So you must have good light and the fastest film or you must use a tripod.

Second, the contrast range between light and dark areas of the print must be higher than the average amateur is used to or likes. A good print for reproduction will probably look too harsh to you at first. "Morning Mist over Gowanus" is out—it will reproduce as a gray mess and if it gets by your editor, the production manager will toss it out.

Third, you must have uncluttered backgrounds unless you want to pay for expensive airbrushing—no trees growing out of the subject's head, no out-of-focus bushes to blend into and distort the outline of your central figure. The simplest way to handle this problem is to put subjects against the sky outdoors, or take the ornaments off the mantle and the pictures off the background wall before exposing indoors.

For helpful guidance and tips from a professional photographer, one good book on camera use and picture developing is *Know Your Camera,* by Alfred Wagg (Wilfred Funk, Inc., New York, 1956). Another, especially good for beginners, is *How to Make Good Pictures,* published by the Eastman Kodak Company, Rochester, New York, and sold in most camera stores for a dollar. Kodak publishes other "how-

to" books, as also does its business rival, Ansco. The instruction sheet that accompanies each roll of film is itself a good picture-taking guide and is worth careful study. Various books on photography should be available in your public library, and one or two would make worthwhile purchases for permanent reference use and study.

Color film is available for most cameras, but it is not customary for publishers to use color plates to illustrate their books, because the cost of color reproductions is high and makes a book expensive. If color photographs are used, however, the reproductions are best made from transparencies (rather than prints), and although 35-millimeter transparencies *might* be acceptable in the absence of any others, most publishers prefer sizes ranging upward from 2¼ by 2¼ inches.

When you have your film developed, ask for contact prints, which will be the same size as your negatives. By examining these prints you can decide which ones can safely be enlarged to the preferred 8-by-10-inch size, and which ones are not suitable for enlarging.

If you do take your own pictures, I suggest that you obtain your contact prints and enlargements from a camera shop rather than the corner drugstore through which most amateurs have their film developed and printed. Explain to the camera shop owner or manager that your enlargements are intended for publication and that careful processing is important.

Also, you can indicate whether you want certain pictures "cropped" before the enlargements are made. For instance, you may have a negative showing a man in the foreground, bending over a laboratory test tube, and a background show-

ing the laboratory wall, clock, or other features which you do not want to appear in the finished print. You can mark the *shiny side* of the negative (not the dull, or emulsion side) with a grease pencil to show exactly what should be cropped, or omitted, from the original picture. Later, the grease pencil marks can easily be rubbed off with a cloth, if desired.

POINT: *If you propose to buy a camera, discuss various makes and models with a qualified professional photographer, whose advice can help you get the type that will best serve your purposes. Invest some time in studying reference books on photography in your public library, or buy one or two for your permanent use.*

PHOTOGRAPHERS FOR HIRE

Some book projects may require a whole series of photographs that can best be made by a professional photographer. If you are not acquainted with such a professional, you will find listings in the Yellow Pages of your telephone directory under "Photographers" and "Photographers, Commercial." Commercial photographers are available for almost any kind of picture-making, at rates ranging from $5 to $25 or more per assignment. For a series of photographs for a book, the photographer would probably charge according to the time spent, the number of pictures taken, and the number of prints ordered.

If you propose to hire a professional photographer, you should explain your project to him and reach a definite understanding about his fee before he does any work for you. You may be able to engage him for a flat rate, or for a stated price per picture, or at a fixed price per day plus the cost of

prints, or perhaps for a share in royalties from the published book in which his pictures will appear (with a credit line for him).

POINT: *Commercial photographers can be hired to take pictures, but if you employ one, have a definite understanding (preferably in writing) in advance as to his rates or fees.*

WHAT ABOUT DRAWINGS AND PAINTINGS?

Illustrations may sometimes include drawings or paintings instead of or in addition to photographs. These, too, are the responsibility of the author, although the services of a professional artist may be needed. My book *The Story of the Kite* has illustrations in four colors, done superbly by John Moment. When my manuscript for that book was accepted, the publisher undertook to find an artist to make the necessary illustrations. On the basis of his sample sketches (which were submitted to me as the author, for my approval), John Moment was given a contract that guaranteed him a share of the royalty customarily paid to an author. In such situations the royalty is divided between author and artist on a mutually agreeable basis, and might range anywhere from equal shares to 2 per cent or 3 per cent for the illustrator, depending upon the nature of the book and the importance and quality of the illustrations. In picture books for little tots for example, the lion's share of the royalty may go to the illustrator. Sometimes the author and illustrator are one and the same person, in which event he would, of course, receive the full royalty. Sometimes the illustrator is paid a flat fee, with no share in the royalties.

If you have some ability in drawing, you might make

sketches yourself. For *Communication,* I made pen-and-ink drawings of certain Egyptian hieroglyphics, ancient Semitic, Greek, and Roman alphabet characters, American Indian picture symbols, Chinese word symbols, and a Roman stylus (writing instrument), a Peruvian *quipu* (knotted ropes), and a goose-quill pen. Patterns for these were found in old books and technical papers, and although I am no Da Vinci, the drawings satisfied the publisher and served to supplement the text.

If you propose to make your own drawings, I suggest you use black India ink on heavy white paper or artist's Bristol board, so that the printed reproductions will be clear and sharp. The drawings may (and probably should) be larger than they will appear in published form, since they will usually be reduced in size to fit pages according to the publisher's layout.

If illustrations in color are called for, even if you are reasonably adept with water colors or oils you should know enough about printing operations to make "overlays" for use in producing separate plates for each color. This should be discussed with your publisher before you undertake to submit colored illustrations for your book.

Even if your drawings or paintings are not suitable for publication, they may be good enough to show a professional artist just what you have in mind. If this is your purpose, the drawings need not be done in ink or in finished form, but can be rough sketches accompanied, if necessary, by marginal notes or suggestions.

POINT: *Drawings or paintings for use as book illustrations are usually done for the author by an artist acceptable to and*

sometimes engaged by the publisher—but if you have the necessary talent and ability, try making your own.

CAPTIONS AND CREDITS

Every photograph you submit with your manuscript should be accurately captioned. Most pictures supplied by public relations people have typewritten captions, but sometimes these are much too lengthy and must be cut drastically. This becomes your job as writer, and you must be sure that your shortened version describes the picture adequately and properly. The publisher will hold you responsible for the caption wording, including the correct spelling of names and places.

Captions may be typewritten on bond paper, the top edge of which is pasted to the back of the photograph so that the typed portion extends below the picture. With this method the part of the paper bearing the caption may be folded up against the photograph itself.

Another way is to type your captions on gummed labels and paste them to the backs of the photos.

Each method avoids the necessity of typing, printing, or writing the captions on the backs of the pictures, a practice that could result in inferior printed reproductions.

In addition to the description of the photograph, your label should carry your own name (and I usually include the title of the book), and a credit line, if necessary; that is, the name of the company or individual who is to be credited with ownership of the original photograph.

In some books the credit line is published under the illustration itself. In others, there may be a listing in the front

or the back of the book identifying all the pictures and their sources.

Accuracy in credit lines is highly important, and whenever you submit a photograph for book use you should indicate *exactly* what credit line is to be published. Often the supplier of the picture will have rubber-stamped the back with an inscription such as: "Please credit the John Jones Company," but if there is no such marking, you should ask what credit line is to be used.

POINT: *Make sure your picture captions are accurate in all respects, and that each photograph carries a proper credit line.*

DON'T TANGLE WITH THE LAW

Certain laws must be considered in the publication of photographs. For example, if you take a photograph of an individual and publish it without his express permission, the individual might be able to sue you in court for an invasion of his privacy. This would not apply, however, to pictures of newsworthy or public figures, such as the President of the United States, or to groups of people in a street scene, where no emphasis is placed upon any one person, or to pictures supplied by public relations or advertising firms for publicity purposes.

Photographs can be copyrighted, just as books and periodicals can, and before you submit photos for publication you should ascertain whether any are protected by copyright. Usually such pictures carry a notice of copyright on the reverse sides. A copyrighted photograph may be lawfully published only with the permission of the copyright owner, who

usually charges a fee for such permission. The copyright owner may be the photographer who took the picture, or a magazine or newspaper in which it first appeared, or it could be a person who hired a photographer to make the picture for him.

If your photographs should include one of a painting owned by a museum or historical society, it is possible that, to get permission for publication, you would have to pay a fee not only to the photographer who took the picture, but also to the owner of the original painting, and give published credit to both.

Sometimes book illustrations include copyrighted charts, graphs, and maps. If you are to use any of these in your book, unless the copyrights have expired, you will have to get permission from, and probably make payment to the copyright owners.

A United States copyright is valid for twenty-eight years and may be renewed for another twenty-eight. More about copyrights is set out in a later chapter.

POINT: *The copyright laws protect photographs and other illustrations, as well as printed texts. Be sure that the pictures you obtain for your book are not protected by copyright— or, if they are, that you get written permission from the copyright owners for their reproduction.*

Remember!

• There are scores of places from which you can obtain good photographs for your book, free of charge. Before you decide that you must buy suitable pictures, try to get the ones you want from industrial companies, advertising

agencies, public relations firms, or state and federal government agencies.

- If necessary, you can buy photographs at low cost from the Library of Congress, the Smithsonian Institution, and the National Archives, all in Washington, D.C. Commercial photographers may also have suitable photographs for sale, but at higher prices.
- Consider the possibility of taking your own photographs, even if it means learning how to use a camera.
- If original drawings or paintings are to be made for use in your book, be sure you understand the arrangements made for the artist's fee; it is possible that the artist will share your royalties. If you have some talent, perhaps you could make your own.
- Make certain that the captions and credit lines on your photographs are absolutely correct.
- Be careful not to infringe the copyright laws by using photographs, charts, graphs, or maps that are protected by copyright.

15

Tantalizing, Goof-proofing, and Indexing

Before you start to type your manuscript in final form, read the rough draft carefully to make sure that words are spelled correctly, statements are expressed succinctly (editors call this "tight writing"), sentences are clear, clichés are eliminated, and that your chapter headings and book title are as catchy or informative as you can make them.

Titles may occasionally lead to word duels between editors and authors. A writer may spend considerable time making a list of possible titles and finally call his book *The Hoptoad and His Mate,* only to have it published under the title *Leapfrog Lovers.*

A tantalizing book or chapter title can make a reader want to find out what follows it. It's a come-on, like a sign over a basket of peanuts that reads "Take one." Who can stop munching with a single peanut? In certain kinds of reference books, however, it may be preferable to play it straight and

use headings that explain content in the fewest possible plain words.

Sometimes I submit six or eight suggested titles with my book outline, hoping that one will appeal to the publisher. In all but one or two instances my titles for sixteen books have been unchanged. In the one or two instances the editors suggested changes that would provide readers with more definite information about the content of the book.

For example, for my book about career opportunities for young people in the field of electronics, I suggested some of the following titles (also using a subtitle to maintain the pat‧ tern of previous career books):

Electrifiers:	*Your Career in Electronics*			
Electroneers:	"	"	"	"
Wireless Wizards:	"	"	"	"
Electro-Team:	"	"	"	"
Electronics and You:	"	"	"	"

At first the publisher thought that *Electrons and You* was satisfactory, but after further consideration it was pointed out that this title, like the others, was too broad and didn't really explain (except for the subtitle) what the book was about. After a discussion we decided to call it simply *Your Career in Electronics*, which is certainly self-explanatory.

POINT: *Consider your book title carefully. Does it accurately reflect the content of the book? If it were among other books on a bookstore counter, would the title tempt a browser to pick it up?*

DO YOUR CHAPTER HEADS HAVE PULLING POWER?

I take as great care with my chapter headings as I do with my book titles, because my books are written to be both informative and enjoyable, and when a prospective reader (or browser) examines the table of contents in the front of the book, I want the chapter headings to arouse his curiosity as well as reflect the contents of the text.

Treasures by the Millions, for instance, is about a museum —and to many people the very thought of a museum evokes visions of lifeless birds and animals, old rocks, dead butterflies, plaster Eskimos, and various relics of the long ago. Here are the chapter headings I used in that book:

CHAPTER 1. TREASURES FOR TWELVE MILLION EYES
CHAPTER 2. THE BENEVOLENT BRITON
CHAPTER 3. STONE STORIES
CHAPTER 4. SECRETS OF THE SKULLS AND BONES
CHAPTER 5. INDIANS!
CHAPTER 6. FINS, FEATHERS AND HAIR
CHAPTER 7. THE PLANT DETECTIVES
CHAPTER 8. EYE FOR INVENTION
CHAPTER 9. WINGS BRAVE AND BOLD
CHAPTER 10. EARTHBOUND SPACE MEN
CHAPTER 11. HARK TO THE PAST
CHAPTER 12. POLITICS, POSTAGE, MONEY AND WAR
CHAPTER 13. BEAUTY AND SEVERAL BEASTS
CHAPTER 14. BACKSTAGE BUSINESS

POINT: *Make your chapter headings as interesting and provocative as you can. Some potential readers (and buyers!)*

may not look beyond your table of contents if you fail to whet
their reading appetites.

GOOF-PROOFING

Now let's suppose that the writing job is done—the publisher has accepted your manuscript and has put it into production. One exciting day you'll receive a set of galley proofs,
which are long, narrow sheets of paper on which your words
appear in print. The text has been set, but it has not yet
been made up into pages. There are, however, ample margins so that you will have room to make whatever revisions
are *necessary* when you proofread your book.

Proofreading is a kind of "goofreading." You read the
printed galleys to be sure the printer has followed your copy
and that there are no misspellings, no mixup of words or
sentences, no errors in numerals—in short, no mistakes at all.

Use accepted proofreaders' marks, such as those that appear
on pages 191-193.

Be careful not to make unnecessary revisions in the galley
proofs. Most contracts provide that if the author makes
changes exceeding a certain percentage of the cost of composition, a deduction in the amount of the excess will be made
from his earnings to take care of them. You should also make
it a point to remember that most books are set by linotype,
which means that each *line* in the book is printed from a
single piece of metal cast by the machine. Perhaps a paragraph in your manuscript is twelve lines long and begins this
way: "Everybody is crazy." When you read the galley proof,
you decide that your statement is too broad because it would
include you, so you insert the word *almost* before *everybody*.

EDITORS' AND PROOFREADERS' MARKS

Size and Style of Type

Mark	Example
wf//	Wrong font (size of style of type) (Repeat stop mark for each additional identical error in same line)
lc//	Lower Case Letter
lc//	Set in LOWER CASE or LOWER CASE
C or cap	capital letter, upper case letter
caps	SET in capitals
lc or u+lc	Cap and Lower Case, Upper and Lower Case
caps or sc	SET IN small CAPITALS
Caps + sc	CAP and SMALL CAPS
rom	Set in roman (or regular) type
ital	*Set in italic (or oblique) type*
rule	Set an underscore
lf	Set in lightface type
bf	**Set in boldface type**
bf ital	***Boldface italic***
b	Superior letter or figure b
2	Inferior letter or figure 2

Position

Mark	Example
] or]	Move to right
[or [	Move to left
⦚	Ragged margin
ctr]	Put in center of line or page [
⊔	Lower (letters or words)
⊓	Elevate (letters or words)
=	Straighten line (horizontally)
||	Align type (vertically)
fl l	Flush left; begin text flush with the left margin
tr	Transpose enclosed in ring matter
tr//	Transpose (order letters of or words)
tr	Rearrange words of order numbers in
tr # or #/	Transpose space or transpose space
run over	Run over to next line (A two-letter di-vision should be avoided.)
run back	Run back to preceding line (This div-ision is incorrect.)
run back	A syllable or short word alone on a line is called a "widow"; it should be elimi-nated

Spacing

Mark	Example
leaded	(Pron. led'əd) Additional space between lines
solid	Not leaded
ld	Insert lead between lines
ℓ ld	Take out lead
⁀	Close up entirely; take out space
less #	Close up partly; leave some space
^ or eq. #	Equalize space between words
space out	More space between words

To avoid costly misunderstandings, all writers should learn to mark manuscript and proofs with standard proofreader's marks. The above will teach you the basic procedure.

thin # or hair #	Thin space where indicated
#	Insert space (or more space)
en #	½-em space or indention
□ *or em #*	Em space or indention

Insertion and Deletion

out—see copy	Insert matter omitted; refer to copy
the/⊂ℓ	Insert marginal additions
℺	Delete—take out and delete
℞	Delete and close up
stet	Let it stand (all matter above dots)

Diacritical Marks; Signs; Symbols

ü	Dieresis or umlaut
é	Acute accent
è	Grave accent
â	Circumflex accent
ç	Cedilla
ñ	Tilde (Spanish); til (Portuguese)
⁀	Use ligature (affix—ffi)
/	Virgule, separatrix, solidus, stop mark, shill mark
✳	Asterisk (*)
⅋	Ampersand (&)
......	Leaders (........)
⊙ # ⊙ # ⊙	Ellipsis (. . .)
	Order of symbols when used for footnote references: * † ‡ § ‖ ¶ #; then double (** †† ...)

Paragraphing

| ¶ | Begin a paragraph |
| *no ¶ or run in* | No paragraph. Run in |

| *fl* | ⌐ No indention |
| *hang in* | Hanging indention (This style shoul have all lines after the first marked t⌐e desired indention.) |

Punctuation

⊙	Period or "full point"
⸲	Comma
⅋ *or* ⊙	Semicolon
⁀ *or* ⊙	Colon
∨ *or* ∨	Apostrophe
∨/∨	Single quotes
∨/∨	Quotation marks, quotes
?/	Question mark, query
!/	Exclamation point
=/	Hyphen
en	En dash
em ¹ *or* H	One-em dash
2/em or 3/em	Two-em dash
(/)	Parentheses (parens)
[/]	Brackets (crotchets)
{/}	Braces

Miscellaneous

e/k	Correct letter or word marked
×///	Replace broken or imperfect type
℥	Reverse upside-down type or cut
⊥ *or* ↓	Push down space (lead) that prints
⒮ⓟ	Spell out (20 gr)
Qy or ?	Query
⌐	Mark-off or break. Start new line
End or 30	End of copy

EXAMPLE OF MARKED PROOF

In choosing the Yankee dialect, I did not act without forethought. It had long

seemed to me that the great voice of American Writing and speaking was a studied

want of simplicity, That we were in danger of coming to look on our mother tongue

as a dead language, to be sought in the grammar and dictionary, rather than in the

heart, and that our only chance of escape was by seeking it at its living sources

among those who were, as Scottowe says of Major general Gibbons, "divinely

illiterate." President Lincoln, the only really great public man whom these later days

have seen, was great also in this, that he was master—witness his speech at Gettysburg

—of a truly masculine English, classic because it was of no special period, and level

at once to the highest and lowest of his countrymen.

—James Russell Lowell, "Introduction
to the Biglow Papers, Second Series"

EXAMPLE OF CORRECTED PROOF

In choosing the Yankee dialect, I did not act without forethought. It had long

seemed to me that the great vice of American writing and speaking was a studied

want of simplicity, that we were in danger of coming to look on our mother-tongue

as a dead language, to be sought in the grammar and dictionary rather than in the

heart, and that our only chance of escape was by seeking it at its living sources

among those who were, as Scottowe says of Major-General Gibbons, "divinely

illiterate." President Lincoln, the only really great public man whom these latter

days have seen, was great also in this, that he was master—witness his speech at

Gettysburg—of a truly masculine English, classic because it was of no special

period, and level at once to the highest and lowest of his countrymen.

—James Russell Lowell, "Introduction

to the Biglow Papers, Second Series"

A minor change, really—but when the galley goes back to the printer, he is compelled to reset not only the first line, but all eleven other lines in that paragraph unless you compensate by deleting another word of similar length in the corrected line or close to it.

Even if you were to change the one word *crazy* to *insane* or *mad,* the whole paragraph might have to be reset. The insertion of a new punctuation mark, such as a comma, means the whole line must be reset. Changes, no matter how minor, are costly in printing time and labor, which is why the writer who makes them must share the costs.

When you return the first galley proofs to the publisher, he will deliver them to the printer to make any necessary corrections, and you will next receive "page proofs." These are also long, narrow, printed sheets, but this time the text is separated into numbered pages just as it will appear in your book. The page proofs offer your final chance to correct any errors.

POINT: *The time to make changes in your text is* before *you submit your manuscript—not when you read proof.*

INDEXING

You will use the page proofs if you are to make the index for your book, although indexes are often compiled by professional indexers through arrangement with the publisher, with the cost charged to the author.

There are advantages in having an index made by a professional indexer. Names and subjects will be spelled correctly and listed in proper alphabetical order. Appropriate cross-references will be made where necessary. If the book

deals with complex scientific matters, or statistics, or some unique or unusual subject, the experienced compiler will know exactly how to prepare the kind of index the book needs, whereas the author might overlook important details if he were to make his own index.

The author, however, knows his own book better than a hired indexer would, and for that reason is sometimes able to produce a better compilation.

If you propose to prepare the index for your book, you will be wise to learn something about indexing before you undertake it. There are several books on this subject that can be most helpful to you. Among them are:

A Manual of Style. University of Chicago Press, 1949.

Indexes and Indexing, by Robert Lewis Collison. E. Benn, London, 1953.

Indexing Books, by Robert Lewis Collison. J. deGraff, New York, 1962.

Indexing Your Book, by Sina Spiker. University of Wisconsin Press, Madison, 1954.

Making An Index, by Gordon Vero Carey. (Vol. III, Cambridge Authors' and Printers' Guides. 14 pages.) Cambridge University Press, London, 1951.

Words Into Type. Based on studies by Marjorie E. Skillin, Robert M. Gay and other authorities. Appleton-Century-Crofts, New York, 1948.

I make my own index for each book, because my books are not so complex that professional indexers are needed. When I receive the page proofs, I use a stack of 3-by-5-inch cards (or paper) for my preliminary listings. I go through the pages, writing in longhand almost all the significant proper names and whatever subjects and cross-references I feel are needed, each with its proper page number. Many names or subject

headings are thus duplicated, of course, and I may make several separate listings of these as I go through the text.

When this preliminary indexing is done, I sort my cards into general alphabetical order, then into proper alphabetical sequence. At this point all duplicate listings come together, and for multilistings the page numbers are shown after a single entry on one 3-by-5 card, in this fashion:

Illustrations, colored, 12, 14, 23.

There would also be another listing for this entry:

Colored illustrations, 12, 14, 23.

When alphabetizing is complete, the listings on the stacks of cards are typewritten double-spaced on letter-size sheets, just as they will appear in the published book. A carbon copy of the finished index is made a part of my carbon copy of the manuscript.

Some publishers find the 3-by-5-inch cards themselves acceptable in place of typewritten pages, provided the card notations are typed or printed clearly, and the cards themselves numbered in proper sequence.

Other writers, of course, may have different indexing methods that produce satisfactory results.

POINT: *If you are not sure how to prepare an index, or if you don't want to do this work yourself, let the publisher arrange with a professional indexer to do it for you. If you intend to make your own index and have had no indexing experience, read a book that explains how to go about this important task.*

THE JACKET AND THE JOY

As part of the preparation of your book, the publisher's promotion department will have asked you for a biographical sketch and perhaps for a photograph of yourself, for publicity purposes and for the jacket of your book.

Perhaps you can provide a personal anecdote that will warm prospective readers to you. Funk & Wagnalls was delighted to use on the jacket of *The Mystery of the Marble Zoo* this anecdote that Mrs. Margaret Goff Clark told the editors:

"I started writing when I was nine and wrote mainly poetry until about eighteen years ago when I met a group of women who shared my interest in writing. We formed the 'Deadliners,' sworn to produce at least one completed manuscript per month or pay a dollar. No one wanted to part with the dollar, so all soon became steady and published writers."

Book jackets are designed by or for the publisher, and you probably won't see yours until about six or seven weeks before the publication date, when you will receive the first magnificent, beautiful, impressive, exciting, bound and jacketed advance copies of your very own book. As the author, you will get anywhere from six to ten *free* copies, depending upon the provisions of your contract. Additional copies can generally be bought by the author at a discount of 50 per cent, unless otherwise specified in the contract.

Just because your book is finally in print, however, *don't throw away any of your notes or other research material.* Keep it all together in some safe place, because there is always a possibility that some reader will raise questions about portions of your work, or even challenge the authenticity of

some statement or other. In such an event you should be in a position to identify the source from which you obtained information on which your statements were based, and you will also be able to provide additional details if they are needed.

POINT: *You can jump for joy when you receive the advance copies of your book, but don't throw away your notes and research materials. You may need them to answer inquiries from readers.*

HELP TO BOOST YOUR OWN BOOK

When your book becomes available to an eager reading public, it is to your advantage to do everything you can to help the publisher promote its sale. You can send a news item to your local newspaper. You can visit bookstores in your town and nearby communities, suggesting that they may want to order copies of the book so that it will be available for purchase by your friends and other interested people. Some bookstores may even want to arrange autographing parties. When your publisher prepares the publication announcements describing the book, you can provide him with a list of names of prospective purchasers to whom copies of the announcements may be sent. Local radio stations usually have programs on which guests are interviewed about activities of interest to the community, and would probably welcome you as a participant in a discussion of your new book. If you belong to a writers' club it is probable that you'll be invited to tell the members about your book and some of the writing problems it entailed. Any other kind of promotion you can generate—in cooperation with the publicity director

of your publisher—will be helpful to you as well as to the publisher and to booksellers who have your book for sale.

POINT: *Do what you can to help your publisher promote the sale of your book.*

Remember!

- Try for a book title that will capture the attention and also indicate what your book is about.
- Take care with your chapter headings. If they don't interest a potential reader or buyer, he may not look at any other part of the book.
- Don't make revisions in the galley proofs unless they are absolutely necessary. Changes can cost you money.
- Decide whether you or a professional indexer should make your book index. If you do it, first get some guidance from a helpful book about indexing.
- When your book is published, don't throw away your research materials. You may need them to back up statements that are questioned by readers.
- Do what you can to help your publisher promote the sale of your book. Every sale means money in your pocket.

16

Contracts and Agents

WHAT'S IN A CONTRACT?

In book publishing, a contract is a printed agreement between author and publisher, binding both parties to its provisions.

For purposes of explanation, let's consider a contract I recently signed. Without giving the detailed language of the agreement, I propose to paraphrase and condense its principal clauses and at the same time present a fair picture of the extent of its coverage. Bear in mind, however, that all contracts are not exactly alike, and that I propose simply to show the potential author the major basics of one formal publishing agreement with a well-established house.

You will, of course, read your own contract very carefully, being sure to query your agent, editor, or your publisher if there is anything in it you don't understand.

Warranty and Indemnity. Here the author warrants that he is the sole proprietor of "the Work" (the manuscript), that it does not infringe any copyright or other law, and that

201

the author will indemnify (insure) the publisher against any claim or suit "arising out of any breach or alleged breach of the foregoing warranties." (Information about copyright law is set out in Chapter 17.)

Rights Granted Territory. The author assigns to the publisher the exclusive right to print, publish, and sell the said Work in English, in book form, throughout the United States and its dependencies, the Philippines, and Canada. (I have an agent, who represents me in other countries. In the event that you do not have an agent, the publisher will represent you "throughout the world.")

Copyright. The publisher agrees to take out the copyright in the name of the author, and to renew it when necessary. Sometimes the contract provides that copyright will be obtained in the name of the publisher. This is a point to be decided between the contract parties. In most cases the question is merely one of form, not of substance.

Manuscript: Character, Due Date, Author's Alterations. This clause is especially important because it specifies the approximate length of the manuscript and the deadline date for its delivery to the publisher. It also provides that the manuscript must be "in content and form satisfactory to the publisher"; that the author will supply all necessary illustrations at his own expense, and an index if required, or will pay costs if the publisher has to obtain them.

The author must also obtain necessary permissions (see Chapter 17) to reprint any "textual or graphic" material, and deliver them in writing with the final manuscript.

Suppose the author fails to deliver his copy by the specified date? The contract allows a ninety-day

extension, and if delivery is not made within that time the publisher may decline to publish the book and the author must return any money advanced by the publisher.

In this same clause, the author agrees not to publish any similar material that will conflict with the sale of the book covered by the contract, without written consent of the publisher.

Also, the author is required to read and return all proofs and to reimburse the publisher for the expense of the author's proof corrections exceeding a stated per cent of cost of composition.

Publication. This clause provides that the publisher shall publish the Work within a given number of months after delivery of the manuscript.

Royalty, U. S. The publisher will pay the author a percentage of the retail selling price of the book. Often the royalty is 10 per cent on a specified number of thousands of copies sold, increasing to 12½ per cent on an additional number of thousands, and to 15 per cent on all copies sold thereafter.

Mail Order. This section provides that sales made by direct mail (that is, not to bookstores or jobbers) will earn a lower royalty, usually 5 per cent.

Reprint Royalties. If there is a reprint of the book, such as a paperbound edition issued by another publisher, the payment for rights to its publication will be divided equally between the author and the original publisher. The same division of earnings will be made if the book is bought by a book club.

Subsidiary Rights. Earnings from subsidiary rights are also shared by publisher and author. Because "subsidiary rights" cover considerable ground, that part of the contract I recently signed defines them this way:

"The following shall be considered as subsidiary rights: serial rights: before and after book publication, dramatic, public reading and other nondramatic performing rights, motion picture rights, translations, digests, abridgments, selections, and anthologies, also mechanical, visual such as microfilm and microprint (excluding motion picture), sound reproducing and recording rights (including television and broadcasting, phonographic, wire and tape recordings but excluding motion pictures), and adaptation of said Work for commercial use. . . ."

Sales Promotion.
The publisher is authorized to permit publication of selections from the book to promote sales, without compensating the author.

Advance.
The amount of the advance to be paid the author by the publisher is typewritten in a blank space on the printed contract form. An "advance" is an advance against all accrued income. That is, whatever amount the publisher pays the author as an advance will be deducted from the author's earnings until it is repaid in full. The agreement is typewritten (not printed) because its provisions are governed by negotiation between publisher and author (or author's agent). An advance may total anywhere from several hundred to several thousand dollars.

Other clauses in the contract relate to such matters as author's free copies, dates of submitting royalty statements, disposition of printing plates, discontinuance of publication after two years or other specified time, arbitration to settle controversies arising from the contract, and options. Options are usually taken by the publisher for the next book-length work of the author.

POINT: *When you sign a book contract, you are bound by its*

provisions. Be sure you understand them clearly before *your signature completes the document.*

WHAT ABOUT A COLLABORATOR?

Some books represent the work of more than one writer, and may be published under the terms of a contract that divides the royalties accordingly. If you should write a book based almost entirely upon information provided by another person, say Roger Whoozis, you might arrange to have its authorship credited to "Roger Whoozis, *as told to* [you] John Scribe."

If it's a real ghost job, perhaps your name would not appear at all.

If you and a partner collaborate in the actual writing of the book, it would be only fair to show that it was written "By John Scribe and Charles Whatsisname."

In most instances of collaboration, the partners agree on the share of the royalties each is to receive, although some ghostwriters set a flat fee for producing a book ostensibly written by someone else. The size of the fee, of course, would depend upon the amount of work to be done and the time consumed.

POINT: *If you work with a collaborating writer, or on an "as-told-to" basis, or as a ghostwriter, have a clear understanding at the outset (preferably in writing) as to how both credit and royalties will be shared, or as to what payment will be made for your services.*

LITERARY AGENT OR NO?

Personally, I prefer to conduct negotiations with publishers through a reputable literary agent, but not all writers feel this way. Some writers like to negotiate directly with editors. The struggling writer who has no agent may find some advantage in submitting his material direct, because he may meet or correspond with editors who can make constructive suggestions about his work, even if they reject it. After a writer has a few articles or stories or a book published, it is probable that agents will approach him as a prospective client.

A competent literary agent knows the market, is personally acquainted with many editors, has had experience in contract negotiations, and is eager to conclude the best possible deal for his author-client because it will also be the best deal for the agent himself.

A literary agent usually receives 10 per cent of the earnings of his client's work. If the author receives a $1,000 advance, the agent collects $100. If the published work sells for $5 a copy and the author's royalty is 10 per cent, or fifty cents, the agent collects five cents per copy. In return, a good agent acts as a kind of manager of the author's literary business, maintains a liaison between author and publishers, seeks new and better outlets for the author's work, frequently makes constructive suggestions for changes in manuscripts before their final submission to publishers, and in general tries in every way to advance the author's interests.

Some literary agents offer to read and criticize manuscripts for "reading fees," as advertised in various magazines. Some of these have been in business a long time, while others are comparative newcomers. Although some sources have sug-

gested that not all of these agents are desirable representatives, I am not in a position to agree or disagree because I have never had dealings with agents who advertise. I do know that there are many agents whose names are rarely, if ever, seen in print and that most of them work on a straight 10 per cent commission basis.

It isn't always easy for an unknown author to find a reputable literary agent who is willing to represent him. Most established agents prefer to handle the work of writers who have a history of published material, because such publication shows that the writers are capable of producing acceptable work. After all, the agent earns his living from sales of books, articles, or stories written by those he represents. His time is money and he cannot afford to waste hours in advising untried writers how to revise and improve amateurish manuscripts. This is one reason some agents say they charge reading fees; these payments reimburse them for time spent on reading and criticism that would otherwise be devoted to sales negotiations for established writers.

The Authors' Guild (6 East 39th Street, New York 16, New York), a branch of The Authors' League of America, provides members with a list of literary agents upon request. The Society of Authors' Representatives (552 Fifth Avenue, New York 36, New York), will provide, on request, a list of its members who subscribe to its practices and principles. The *Literary Market Place* is also a source to consult. A list of agents is published in *The Writer's Market,* a comprehensive grouping of magazine and book publishers and television and play producers, with descriptions of their requirements.

All this boils down to the fact that if you have had short stories or articles published in magazines, or if you have had a book published, you should be able to find a reputable

literary agent who will represent you. If you have not had anything published anywhere, but have written a salable manuscript, you still may be able to interest an agent.

POINT: *A reputable literary agent can be helpful to a writer who can produce salable manuscripts. No matter how efficient an agent may be, however,* he cannot sell inferior writing. *The writer's work must speak for itself.*

LIBEL

Be sure your manuscript contains no "libelous material." Any statement injuring the reputation of a living person is potentially libelous. Which does not mean that you can speak ill of the dead with impunity. Nor can you invade the privacy of a living person. If you are doubtful, consult a lawyer.

Remember!

- Before you sign any contract, read it carefully and be sure you understand it clearly. If any provisions are hazy or puzzling to you, discuss them with your editor, publisher, or agent if you have one.
- If you can produce salable manuscripts, a literary agent can be helpful to you in marketing them and protecting your rights as an author. If you approach an agent to handle your work, satisfy yourself that the agent is reputable, works on a commission basis, and is not merely selling manuscript criticism for "reading fees."

17

Copyrights and Copycats

WHAT'S A COPYRIGHT?

A copyright is just what the word implies. It's a right that governs copying. That is, it empowers its owner to grant or withhold permission for someone else to copy his written or pictorial work.

Literary properties—published books, articles, stories, plays, poems, songs—are usually copyrighted and may not lawfully be copied without the permission of the copyright owner.

The federal copyright laws (Title 17, U.S. Code of Laws) are so complex and involved that Congress, in 1955, authorized the Copyright Office to make studies leading to a general revision of these laws. In July, 1961, the Register of Copyrights submitted a report to the Judiciary Committee of the House of Representatives, making tentative recommendations for such a revision. This report explains copyright as follows:

In essence, copyright is the right of an author to control the reproduction of his intellectual creation. As long as he keeps his work in his sole possession, the author's absolute control is a physical fact. When he discloses the work to others, however, he makes it possible for them to reproduce it. Copyright is a legal device to give him the right to control its reproduction after it has been disclosed.

Copyright does not preclude others from using the ideas or information revealed by the author's work. It pertains to the literary, musical, graphic, or artistic form in which the author expresses intellectual concepts. It enables him to prevent others from reproducing his individual expression without his consent. But anyone is free to create his own expression of the same concepts, or to make practical use of them, as long as he does not copy the author's form of expression.

Copyright is generally regarded as a form of property, but is property of a unique kind. It is intangible and incorporeal. The thing to which the property right attaches—the author's intellectual work—is incapable of possession except as it is embodied in a tangible article such as a manuscript, book, record, or film. The tangible articles containing the work may be in the possession of many persons other than the copyright owner, and they may use the work for their own enjoyment, but copyright restrains them from reproducing the work without the owner's consent.

A copy of the 160-page report may be purchased for forty-five cents from the Superintendent of Documents, Government Printing Office, Washington, 25, D.C. The title is *Copyright Law Revision*.

A completed book (or article, or short story) manuscript is protected by "common law copyright," which means that it belongs solely to the author (and his lawful heirs), unless he

assigns ownership to other persons, and until it is published. Upon publication, the work is formally copyrighted according to federal law *if* it meets the necessary legal requirements. For example, the word *copyright* and/or the symbol ©, with the year of publication and name of the copyright owner, should appear on the reverse side of a book's title page, like this: "Copyright © 1964 by Harry Edward Neal."

If this required notice is omitted, or if it is not in the specified place, the book may fall into the "public domain," meaning that it can be copied or reproduced without restriction.

A book carrying the proper copyright notice in the proper place is given statutory copyright upon publication, but is not automatically registered in the copyright office. Registration requires that an application form be executed (usually by the publisher) and sent to the Register of Copyrights, Library of Congress, Washington 25, D.C., with the necessary fee ($4.00) and two copies of the published work.

When a book is copyrighted, its entire contents are protected. That is, if the book includes pictures, charts, maps, graphs, statistical tables, drawings, or other graphic reproductions, they are all covered by the copyright.

Copyright protection extends to personal letters, such as those you write to or receive from your wife, husband, son, or brother. They are the lawful property of the letter-writers —not the addressees or physical holders. If you wanted to include in your book a letter written to you by a friend or relative, you could not lawfully do so without his permission.

Songs or other musical compositions, photographs, plays, and speeches may be officially copyrighted *before* publication by filing copies of the manuscripts or pictures in the copyright office and making the necessary application.

A copyright is valid for twenty-eight years, and if it is registered in the copyright office it may be renewed for another twenty-eight years. In other words, a book or other literary property copyrighted more than fifty-six years ago is now definitely in the public domain.

If a book was copyrighted in 1930, say, the first copyright period of twenty-eight years would have expired in 1958, but the copyright notice (1930) would not indicate whether it had been renewed for another twenty-eight years (to 1986). You could get this information only from the copyright office, which would charge a fee for making the necessary file search.

POINT: *A copyright is a legal device that gives its owner the right to control the reproduction of all or parts of his creation. Common law copyright protects your manuscript until publication, when it will get statutory copyright protection if all legal requirements have been met.*

DON'T PILFER, GET PERMISSION

Writers of nonfiction books and articles usually obtain at least some of their facts from the published works of other writers (who obtained theirs that way, too). If these works have been copyrighted, they cannot lawfully be copied without the permission of the copyright owner, unless they are in the public domain—except for what the courts have called "fair use."

This is a term that can result in all sorts of squabbling, because there is no hard and fast definition of what constitutes "fair use." I can't give a solid answer to the question: "How extensively can I copy another's work as 'fair use,' without the copyright owner's permission?" A lawyer could

make a calculated guess, but he certainly wouldn't attempt to do so without seeing the copyrighted work, the amount of material to be excerpted from it, and the way you're going to use it.

From a common-sense viewpoint, if you wanted to copy four lines (50 per cent) of an eight-line poem without permission, it's likely that this would be considered more than fair use, and that you would be guilty of infringement. Even a single line of verse, or a line from a song, might constitute infringement of copyright. If, however, you proposed to copy a twenty-line paragraph from a 400-page book on American history in order to illustrate a point in a work of your own, this would probably be accepted as fair use, so long as you acknowledged the author and the source in a footnote or in some way.

If you wrote a book about African violets, and quoted enough material from another book on that subject to harm the sales of that book, while increasing sales of your own, you would hardly be making fair use of the other writer's property. You could be in bad trouble.

My Funk & Wagnalls *Standard College Dictionary* defines the word *fair* as *just, according to rules and principles, legitimate* (as a *fair question*). Legal technicalities aside, a reasonable lay definition of "fair use" (with respect to copying from copyrighted works) might be: Use of the protected material to such a minor degree that no injustice, impairment of value, or disadvantage, accrues to the copyright owner.

The best of all answers is, "Don't fool around with fair use. If you want to quote *anything* from copyrighted works, get the permission of the copyright owners."

POINT: *You* might *be able to quote copyrighted material on the basis of "fair use," but it's best to be on the safe side and get written permission from the copyright owner.*

HOW DO YOU GET PERMISSION?

If you propose to use something from a published book, the copyright notice at the front of that book will tell you the name of the copyright owner. You may write to him in care of the book's publisher, or directly to the publisher, incorporating in your letter the exact material you want to use, and asking for written authority to use it. You should also explain what your book is about and how the requested material will fit into it.

If the book is copyrighted in the name of the author, and if he is not available to consider your request, it is probable that the publisher will be able to grant the necessary permission on the author's behalf, or can put you in touch with the author's attorney or agent, who can give you the authorization you need.

Although permission to copy is sometimes given without charge, it is quite possible that such permission will be forthcoming only upon payment of some amount specified by the copyright owner or his representative. There is no set scale for such charges, and the size of the fee is governed only by the discretion of the copyright owner. In most instances it is reasonable, although if an anthology is in preparation the total permission costs could be very high.

Fees for permission are paid by the requesting writer, not by the publisher. For this reason, you should not seek needed permission until you have a signed contract for your book in

which the authorized material is to be used. You should include this material in your manuscript when you submit it, on the assumption that you will be able to get the permission if a contract is drawn. It is possible, of course, that you will *not* get the authority, and it is therefore advisable for you to have some other material in mind to substitute for the quoted passage.

Of course, if you are planning a book to be made up largely of reprinted material, you will want to query the publishers—without committing yourself—so that you can figure your budget.

When an excerpt is quoted by permission, it should be marked with an asterisk and footnoted. The footnote should be approximately in this form:

> * From *What To Do In Case of Peace,* by Charles Dugall. Copyright © 1964, Bomm & Co., New York. Quote by permission.

Or you can list acknowledgments to be printed together on the copyright page. The copyright page of any anthology will show you how to set this up. This method is certainly simpler, especially if you have a long list of credits. However, remember that not only the wording of the credit line but also the place at which it is to appear are governed by the copyright holders and some of them insist that it appear on the page that carries the quoted material.

POINT: *Permission to copy should be sought from the copyright owner, his publisher, or his agent. Set out exactly what portion of his work you want to quote, and explain how it will be used in your book. Permission may require payment of a fee—by you.*

PROTECTING YOUR OWN COPYRIGHT

As author of a duly copyrighted book or other work, you should be alert for any infringement of that work. If the publisher of your book learns of such an infringement, he will notify you promptly. If you decide to take legal action against the infringer, your publisher may or may not join you; but if he elects to refrain, he cannot prevent you from acting alone.

If the publisher decided to bring suit against an alleged infringer of your book, you might be the one to withdraw, but your lack of participation in the action would not prevent the publisher from proceeding on his own.

In most instances, a book contract will include a clause defining author-publisher obligations relating to infringements of copyright.

If an infringement suit involving your copyrighted work is decided in favor of you and your publisher, the amount of damages will be fixed by the court. In addition, if the offender (the infringer) should be tried and convicted for his violation of the copyright laws, he could be sentenced to a maximum of one year in a federal prison and payment of a $1,000 fine.

POINT: *If your copyrighted work is infringed, confer with your publisher about legal action to be taken. A publisher will probably have had more experience than you in such matters and should be able to offer sound advice. If he recommends against a suit, you are still at liberty to proceed by yourself unless your contract has contrary provisions.*

CAN PLAIN FACTS BE COPYRIGHTED?

Facts and ideas, in themselves, cannot be copyrighted. It is the language used to express them, the manner in which they are developed, and the way in which they are arranged or presented that the copyright protects. Suppose one book contained the passage: "Christopher Columbus, of Genoa, commanding a fleet of three small ships—the Niña, the Pinta, and the Santa Maria—sailed across what was called 'the dark sea' in 1492 and discovered the New World."

You could lawfully use the fact that Christopher Columbus made his voyage of discovery in 1492, and you could name his three ships, so long as you did not copy the language and sequence of the original: "In 1492, three small ships sailed an unknown sea and heaved anchor in a virgin land that was to become a new world. The ships were named the Niña, the Pinta, and the Santa Maria. The courageous explorer who dared the crossing was a Genoese named Christopher Columbus."

Of course, if it is *certain* that the copyright has expired on some particular book, you may copy verbatim excerpts from that book without violating the law. Even then, simple courtesy demands that you identify the book, author, and publisher.

POINT: *Facts and ideas can't be copyrighted. If you obtain and use facts from a copyrighted source, make sure you do not set them out in the same wording and sequence. Your presentation must be indicative of your original thinking and planning.*

There are so many aspects and complexities of the copy-

right laws that whole books have been written about them. For basic guidance, however, there is a useful forty-page booklet, *A Copyright Guide,* by Harriet F. Pilpel and Morton David Goldberg (published in 1960 and revised in 1963 by the R. R. Bowker Company in cooperation with The Copyright Society of the U.S.A.). Copies may be purchased for $3 each from the R. R. Bowker Company (1180 Avenue of the Americas, New York 36, N. Y.).

For a study of the copyright laws themselves, for $2 you may buy a 150-page loose-leaf book, *Copyright Enactments: Laws Passed in the United States Since 1783 Relating to Copyright,* from the Superintendent of Documents, Government Printing Office, Washington 25, D.C. (This is a compilation of the laws on copyright and related matters that have been enacted from 1783 through 1962. In ordering the book, mention the title and Code No. 35-V.)

Remember!

- A copyright gives its owner the right to control reproduction of all or parts of his creation. A manuscript is protected by common law copyright until it is published, and then by statutory copyright, if it meets the proper legal requirements.
- You *might* be able to quote copyrighted material and claim "fair use." If there's any doubt whatever, get written permission from the copyright owner. It's much safer!
- Permission to reprint may require the payment of a fee— by you.
- If your own copyright is infringed, you or your publisher

may institute legal action against the infringer, with or without the active participation of both.

• Plain facts can't be copyrighted—only the manner in which they are expressed and arranged.

18

Format and Fortitude

MANUSCRIPT MAKEUP

As a workshop leader at writers' conferences, I learned that many beginning writers were not familiar with accepted manuscript format.

A manuscript should be typewritten double- or triple-spaced with a black ribbon on one side of a good grade of white bond paper, preferably Substance 20. The left margin should be at least $1\frac{1}{2}$ inches wide, the right at least 1 inch, with an inch or more at both top and bottom of each page. The margins provide space for editorial instructions to the printer.

For my book manuscripts I type the book title in the center of one page, all in capital letters and without under-lining or quotation marks, followed by my name, like this:

FARMING AIN'T NO FUN
By
Harry Edward Neal

If I were to use a pen name, it would be typewritten under the word *by,* and this is the name that would appear on the published book.

In the upper left corner of the title page I write my (true) name and address. In the upper right corner I indicate the *approximate* number of words in the book. For this estimate I strike an average of the number of words per line, multiplied by the average number of lines per page, multiplied by the number of pages. For instance, an average of twelve words per line and twenty-five lines per page represents 300 words per page. If there are 200 pages there will be approximately 60,000 words.

On page 1, about six lines from the top, indented five spaces, I type in capitals the word PREFACE. I usually introduce my books with a preface in which I include significant sidelights about the contents and give thanks and name-credits to individuals or organizations whose information has been helpful in my research.

On another page I type the centered heading CONTENTS, under which I list chapter numbers and chapter titles.

On the page where Chapter 1 begins, I repeat my full name in the upper left corner and repeat the book title and approximate wordage in the upper right corner. CHAPTER 1 is centered about six lines from the top.

On all subsequent pages I type my last name in the upper left corner, the page number at top center, and one or two key words from the book title in the upper right corner, like this:

NEAL   — 4 —   NONFICTION

If a page is misplaced in the course of manufacturing the

book, the key words identify the manuscript to which it belongs.

A book manuscript should be mailed in a sturdy container, such as the box in which new typewriter paper is packaged. Pages should not be stapled or clipped together, although I sometimes put a thin rubber band around them.

Postal regulations permit the mailing of typewritten manuscripts within the U.S. at the rate of ten cents for the first pound or fraction thereof, and five cents for each additional pound or fraction, provided the package is plainly marked with the words EDUCATIONAL MATERIALS. A first-class letter may be enclosed with the manuscript, or attached to the outside of the package, if extra postage is affixed at the regular first-class rate of five cents per ounce or fraction of an ounce, and if the package is also marked with the words FIRST CLASS LETTER ENCLOSED.

If an unsolicited book manuscript is mailed to a publisher, the author should enclose return postage. If the manuscript is rejected the publisher *might* pay return postage, but more likely it would be sent back by express collect.

If you write in longhand and aren't a capable typist, you can hire someone to type your manuscript. Advertisements in writers' magazines indicate that the charge for such work ranges from fifty to seventy-five cents or more per thousand words, with one carbon copy. This fee is based primarily on short stories and magazine articles, and most typists would undoubtedly quote special rates for book-length manuscripts.

POINT: *Before you submit any manuscript to a publisher, be sure it is typewritten and is neat and professional in appearance.*

Manuscript format, copyrights, stories, articles, books, agents, and other aspects of the writing business are discussed in depth at many writers' conferences held throughout the United States every year. Such conferences offer writers—both beginners and professionals—an opportunity to meet and talk shop, but of special importance is the fact that conference faculties generally consist of working authors in various literary fields, prepared to share their knowledge with newcomers to the writing business.

The writers' conference permits conferees to submit manuscripts to faculty members for constructive criticism (included in the conference fee), and this is one way in which a beginner can get valuable professional help on his writing project. Also, he will have an opportunity to talk face to face with editors, publishers, and (sometimes) literary agents who visit the conferences as guest speakers.

Most conferences charge very nominal rates for tuition, room, and board. I have lectured and conducted fiction and nonfiction workshops at several of these conclaves, and have always found them enjoyable and stimulating.

Schedules of conferences are usually advertised in magazines (*The Writer, Writer's Digest, Author & Journalist, Saturday Review*) every spring.

Courses in fiction and nonfiction writing are offered by some colleges, by community adult-education groups, by some institutions such as the Y.M.C.A. or Y.W.C.A., by writers conducting private classes, and by various correspondence schools. Personal participation in a writing class can be helpful, because it requires the completion of writing assign-

ments which will be criticized by the instructor, it offers the opportunity to hear, read, or discuss what other class members have written, and it serves to encourage one's determination to keep writing.

In some towns and cities where no formal classes are available, individuals who are interested in writing organize writers' clubs and hold weekly meetings in private homes, or, if the group is large, in some community hall. If there is no such group in your town, perhaps you would want to think about organizing one.

POINT: *Writers' conferences, writers' magazines, classes, and books for writers can all be helpful to the apprentice and even to the master. They can teach a great deal about techniques, about the mechanics of writing, but they cannot make any man or woman into a professional writer.*

PERSEVERANCE PAYS OFF

Fifteen minutes of daily writing can produce a book within a year at most. One double-spaced typewritten page per day (excluding Saturdays and Sundays) for fifty weeks will total about 250 typed pages, or around 75,000 words—more than enough for a book. This, of course, does not take into account whatever time must be spent in research, but much can be done by correspondence or telephone or in the local library. After all, the man or woman who sets out to write a nonfiction book must expect to devote time to the collection of needed information unless he or she is an authority who can write at length on the basis of his own knowledge and experience.

You don't know what to write about? You might start by

keeping a daily journal of your own activities, because writing *regularly* will give you a facility with words—and these, of course, are a writer's stock in trade. The only way anyone ever learned to write professionally was by putting words on paper—thousands and thousands of words. There is no short cut, no other way.

POINT: *If you want to be a writer*—WRITE!

Remember!

- Give your typewritten manuscripts a professional appearance.
- Consider attending a writers' conference or a class in writing.
- Write something every day.
- Write.

Index

Index